2nd Workshop on Linking Models of Lexical, Sentential and Discourse-level Semantics (LSDSem 2017)

Valencia, Spain
3 April 2017

ISBN: 978-1-5108-3866-6

Introduction

Welcome to the 2nd Workshop on Linking Models of Lexical, Sentential and Discourse-level Semantics.

This workshop takes place for the second time, with the goal of gathering and showcasing theoretical and computational approaches to joint models of semantics, and applications that incorporate multi-level semantics. Improved computational models of semantics hold great promise for applications in language technology, be it semantics at the lexical level, sentence level or discourse level. This year we have an additional focus on the comprehensive understanding of narrative structure in language. Recently a range of tasks have been proposed in the area of learning and applying commonsense/procedural knowledge. Such tasks include, for example, learning prototypical event sequences and event participants, modeling the plot structure of novels, and resolving anaphora in Winograd schemas.

This year's workshop further includes a shared task, the Story Cloze Test–a new evaluation for story understanding and script learning. This test provides a system with a four-sentence story and two possible endings, and the system must choose the correct ending to the story. Successful narrative understanding (getting closer to human performance of 100%) requires systems to link various levels of semantics to commonsense knowledge. A total of eight systems participated in the shared task, with a variety of approaches including end-to-end neural networks, feature-based regression models, and rule-based methods. The highest performing system achieves an accuracy of 75.2%, a substantial improvement over the previous state-of-the-art of 58.5%.

We received 19 papers in total, out of which we accepted 13. These papers are presented as talks at the workshop as well as in a poster session. In addition, the workshop program features talks from two invited speakers who work on different aspects of semantics. The day will end with a discussion session where invited speakers and workshop participants further discuss the insights gained during the workshop.

Our program committee consisted of 23 researchers who provided constructive and thoughtful reviews. This workshop would not have been possible without their hard work. Many thanks to you all. Finally, a huge thank you to all the authors who submitted papers to this workshop and made it a big success.

Michael, Nasrin, Nate, and Annie

Organizers:

Michael Roth, University of Illinois and Saarland University
Nasrin Mostafazadeh, University of Rochester
Nate Chambers, United States Naval Academy
Annie Louis, University of Essex

Program Committee:

Omri Abend, The Hebrew University of Jerusalem
Tim Baldwin, University of Melbourne
Johan Bos, University of Groningen
Ido Dagan, Bar Ilan University
Vera Demberg, Saarland University
Katrin Erk, University of Texas at Austin
Anette Frank, Heidelberg University
Aurelie Herbelot, University of Trento
Graeme Hirst, University of Toronto
Sebastian Martschat, Heidelberg University
Philippe Muller, Toulouse University
Beata Beigman Klebanov, Educational Testing Service
Hwee Tou Ng, National University of Singapore
Vincent Ng, University of Texas at Dallas
Jan Snajder, University of Zagreb
Swapna Somasundaran, Educational Testing Service
Caroline Sporleder, Göttingen University
Christian Stab, Technische Universität Darmstadt
Manfred Stede, University of Potsdam
Joel Tetreault, Grammarly
Lucy Vanderwende, Microsoft Research
Luke Zettlemoyer, University of Washington
Heike Zinsmeister, Universität Hamburg

Invited Speakers:

Johan Bos, University of Groningen
Hannah Rohde, University of Edinburgh

Table of Contents

Conference Program

Monday, April 3, 2017

09:30–11:00 **Morning Session**

9:30–9:40 *Introduction*
Michael Roth

9:40–10:40 *Invited talk: Integrating Lexical and Discourse Semantics in the Parallel Meaning Bank*
Johan Bos

10:40–11:00 *Inducing Script Structure from Crowdsourced Event Descriptions via Semi-Supervised Clustering*
Lilian Wanzare, Alessandra Zarcone, Stefan Thater and Manfred Pinkal

11:00–11:30 *Coffee break*

11:30–12:40 **Pre-lunch Session**

11:30–11:50 *A Consolidated Open Knowledge Representation for Multiple Texts*
Rachel Wities, Vered Shwartz, Gabriel Stanovsky, Meni Adler, Ori Shapira, Shyam Upadhyay, Dan Roth, Eugenio Martínez-Cámara, Iryna Gurevych and Ido Dagan

11:50–12:05 *Event-Related Features in Feedforward Neural Networks Contribute to Identifying Causal Relations in Discourse*
Edoardo Maria Ponti and Anna Korhonen

12:05–12:25 *Stance Detection in Facebook Posts of a German Right-wing Party*
Manfred Klenner, Don Tuggener and Simon Clematide

12:25–12:40 *Behind the Scenes of an Evolving Event Cloze Test*
Nathanael Chambers

12:40–14:30 **Lunch Break**

14:30–15:30   Post-lunch Session

14:30–14:45   *LSDSem 2017 Shared Task: The Story Cloze Test*
Nasrin Mostafazadeh, Michael Roth, Annie Louis, Nathanael Chambers and James Allen

14:45–15:00   *Story Cloze Task: UW NLP System*
Roy Schwartz, Maarten Sap, Ioannis Konstas, Leila Zilles, Yejin Choi and Noah A. Smith

15:00–15:15   *LSDSem 2017: Exploring Data Generation Methods for the Story Cloze Test*
Michael Bugert, Yevgeniy Puzikov, Andreas Rücklé, Judith Eckle-Kohler, Teresa Martin, Eugenio Martínez-Cámara, Daniil Sorokin, Maxime Peyrard and Iryna Gurevych

15:15–15:30   *Sentiment Analysis and Lexical Cohesion for the Story Cloze Task*
Michael Flor and Swapna Somasundaran

15:30–16:30   Poster Session (all papers)

15:30–16:30   *Resource-Lean Modeling of Coherence in Commonsense Stories*
Niko Schenk and Christian Chiarcos

15:30–16:30   *An RNN-based Binary Classifier for the Story Cloze Test*
Melissa Roemmele, Sosuke Kobayashi, Naoya Inoue and Andrew Gordon

15:30–16:30   *IIT (BHU): System Description for LSDSem'17 Shared Task*
Pranav Goel and Anil Kumar Singh

15:30–16:30   *Story Cloze Ending Selection Baselines and Data Examination*
Todor Mihaylov and Anette Frank

16:00–16:30   *Coffee Break*

16:30–18:00   Afternoon Session   xi

16:30–17:30   *Invited talk: Using Story Continuations to Model Discourse Expectations*
Hannah Rohde

17:30–18:00   *Open Discussion*

Inducing Script Structure from Crowdsourced Event Descriptions via Semi-Supervised Clustering

Lilian D. A. Wanzare   **Alessandra Zarcone**   **Stefan Thater**   **Manfred Pinkal**

Universität des Saarlandes
Saarland, 66123, Germany
{wanzare,zarcone,stth,pinkal}coli.uni-saarland.de

Abstract

We present a semi-supervised clustering approach to induce script structure from crowdsourced descriptions of event sequences by grouping event descriptions into paraphrase sets (representing event types) and inducing their temporal order. Our model exploits semantic and positional similarity and allows for flexible event order, thus overcoming the rigidity of previous approaches. We incorporate crowdsourced alignments as prior knowledge and show that exploiting a small number of alignments results in a substantial improvement in cluster quality over state-of-the-art models and provides an appropriate basis for the induction of temporal order. We also show a coverage study to demonstrate the scalability of our approach.

1 Introduction

During their daily social interactions, people make seamless use of knowledge about standardized event sequences (*scripts*) describing types of everyday activities, or *scenarios*, such as GOING TO THE RESTAURANT or BAKING A CAKE (Schank and Abelson, 1977; Barr and Feigenbaum, 1981). Script knowledge is often triggered by the broader discourse context and guides expectations in text understanding and makes missing events and referents in a discourse accessible. For example, if we hear someone say "I baked a cake on Sunday. I decorated it with buttercream icing!", our script knowledge allows us to infer that the speaker must have *mixed the ingredients, turned on the oven*, etc., even if these events are not explicitly mentioned. Script knowledge is relevant for the computational modeling of various kinds of cogni-

tive abilities and has the potential to support NLP tasks such as anaphora resolution (Rahman and Ng, 2011), discourse relation detection, semantic role labeling, temporal order analysis, and applications such as text understanding (Cullingford, 1977; Mueller, 2004), information extraction (Rau et al., 1989), question answering (Hajishirzi and Mueller, 2012).

Several methods for the automatic acquisition of script knowledge have been proposed. Seminal work by Chambers and Jurafsky (2008; 2009) provided methods for the unsupervised wide-coverage extraction of script knowledge from large text corpora. However, texts typically only mention small parts of a script, banking on the reader's ability to infer missing script-related events. The task is therefore challenging, and the results are quite noisy.

The work presented in this paper follows the approach proposed in Regneri et al. (2010) (henceforth "RKP") who crowdsourced scenario descriptions by asking people how they typically carry out a particular activity. The collected event sequence descriptions provide generic descriptions of a given scenario (e.g. BAKING A CAKE) in concise telegram style (Fig. 1a). Based on these crowdsourced event sequence descriptions or ESDs, RKP extracted high-quality script knowledge for a variety of different scenarios, in the form of temporal script graphs (Fig. 1b). Temporal script graphs are partially ordered structures whose nodes are sets of alternative descriptions denoting the same event type, and whose edges express temporal precedence.

While RKP employ Multiple Sequence Alignment (MSA) (Durbin et al., 1998), we use a *semi-supervised clustering approach* for script structure induction. The choice of MSA was motivated by the effect of positional information on the detection of scenario-specific paraphrases: event de-

1

Proceedings of the 2nd Workshop on Linking Models of Lexical, Sentential and Discourse-level Semantics, pages 1–11,
Valencia, Spain, April 3, 2017. ©2017 Association for Computational Linguistics

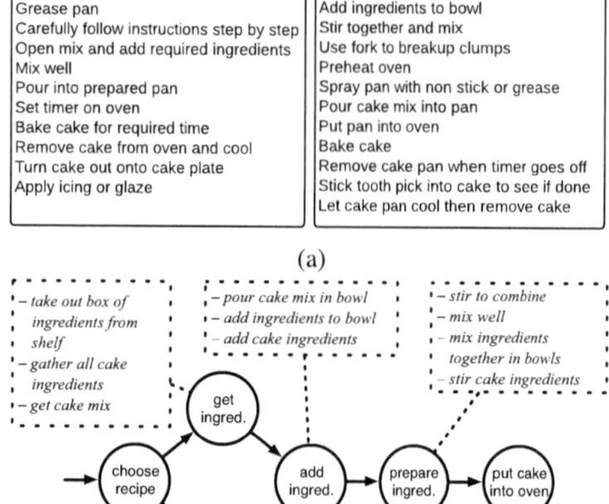

Figure 1: Example ESDs (a) and induced script structure (b) for the BAKING A CAKE scenario from Wanzare et al. (2016)

scriptions occurring in similar positions in ESDs tend to denote the same event type. However, MSA makes far too strong an assumption about the temporal ordering information in the ESDs. It does not allow for crossing edges and thus must assume a fixed and invariable order, while the ordering of events in a script is to some degree flexible (e.g., one can *preheat the oven* before or after *mixing ingredients*). We propose clustering as an alternative method to overcome the rigidity of the MSA approach, and use a distance measure based on both semantic similarity and positional similarity information, making our clustering algorithm sensitive to ordering information, while allowing for order variation in the scripts.

Clustering accuracy depends on the reliability of similarity estimates, but scenario-specific paraphrase relations are often based on scenario-specific functional equivalence, which cannot be easily determined using semantic similarity, even if complemented with positional information. For example in the FLYING IN AN AIRPLANE scenario, it is challenging for any semantic similarity measure to predict that *walk up the ramp* and *board plane* refer to the same event, as the broader discourse context would suggest. To address this issue, we propose a semi-supervised approach, capitalizing on previous work by Klein et

al. (2002). Semi-supervised approaches to clustering have shown that performance can be enhanced by incorporating prior knowledge in the form of a small number of instance-level constraints. We automatically identify event descriptions that are likely to cause alignment problems (called *outliers*), crowdsource alignments for these items and incorporate them as instance-level relational seeds into the clustering process.

Lastly, a main concern with the approach in RKP is scalability: temporal script graphs are created scenario-wise in a bottom-up fashion. They represent only fragments of the rich amount of script knowledge people use in everyday communication. In this paper we address this concern with the first assessment of the coverage of existing script resources, and an estimate of the concrete costs for their extension.

2 Data

We will now introduce the resources used in our study, namely the datasets of ESDs, the gold standards and the crowdsourced alignments between event descriptions.

Datasets and gold standards. Three large crowdsourced collections of activity descriptions in terms of ESDs are available: the OMICS corpus (Gupta and Kochenderfer, 2004), the SMILE corpus (Regneri et al., 2010) and DeScript corpus (Wanzare et al., 2016). Sections 3-4 of this paper focus on a subset of ESDs for 14 scenarios from SMILE and OMICS, with on average 29.9 ESDs per scenario. In RKP, in the follow-up studies by Frermann et al. (2014) and Modi and Titov (2014) as well as in the present study, 4 of these scenarios were used as development set and 10 as test set.

RKP provided two gold standard datasets for this subset: the *RKP paraphrase dataset* contains judgments for 60 event description pairs per scenario, the *RKP temporal order dataset* contains 60 event description pairs that are separately annotated in both directions, for a total of 120 datapoints per scenario. In order to directly evaluate our models for clustering quality, we also created a *clustering gold standard* for the RKP test set, adopting the experimental setup in Wanzare et al. (2016): we asked three trained students of computational linguistics to annotate the scenarios with gold standard alignments between event descriptions in different ESDs referring to the same event[1]. Every ESD was fully aligned with every other ESD in the same scenario. Based on the alignments, we derived gold clusters by grouping the event descriptions into gold paraphrase sets (17 clusters per scenario on average, ranging from 10 to 23).

In addition, we used a subset of 10 scenarios with 25 ESDs each from DeScript, for which Wanzare et al. (2016) provided gold clusters, to evaluate our models and to demonstrate that our method is independent of the specific choice of scenarios.

Crowdsourced alignments. To provide seed data for the semi-supervised clustering algorithm, we crowdsourced alignments between event descriptions, following the procedure in Wanzare et al. (2016). First, we identified challenging cases of event descriptions (called *outliers*), which we expected to be particularly informative and help improve clustering accuracy. To this purpose, an (unsupervised) clustering system (Affinity Propagation, see below) was run with varying parameter settings. Those event descriptions whose nearest neighbors changed clusters across different runs of the system were then identified as outliers (see Wanzare et al. (2016) for more details). A complementary type of seed data was obtained by selecting event descriptions that did not change cluster membership at all (called *stable cases*).

In a second step, groups of selected descriptions (outliers and stable cases) in their original ESD were presented to workers in a Mechanical Turk experiment, paired with a target ESD. The workers were asked to select a description in the target ESD denoting the same script event (e.g. for BAKING A CAKE: *pour into prepared pan → pour cake mix into pan*). We aimed at collecting two sets of high-quality seeds based on outliers and stable cases, respectively, each summing up to 3% of the links required for a total alignment between all pairs of scenario-specific ESDs (6% links in total). To guarantee high quality, we accepted only items where three (out of up to four) annotators agree. We checked the annotators' reliability by comparing their alignments for stable cases against the gold standard and rejected the work on 3% of the annotators.

We collected alignments for 20 scenarios: for the test scenarios of the SMILE+OMICS dataset, and for those in the clustering gold standard of De-

Script. For the latter, a collection of alignment data was already available, but considerably differed in size between scenarios and was in general to small for our purposes.

3   Model

We first present a semi-supervised clustering method to induce script events from ESDs using crowdsourced alignments as seeds (Section 3.1). In Section 3.2, we describe how we calculate the underlying distance matrix based on semantic and positional similarity information. In Section 3.3, we describe the induction of temporal order for the script events, which turns the set of script events into a temporal script graph (TSG).

3.1   Semi-supervised Clustering

We use the crowdsourced alignments between event descriptions as instance-level relational seeds for clustering, more specifically as *must-link constraints*, requiring that the linked items should go into one cluster. We incorporate the constraints into the clustering process following the method in Klein et al. (2002): that is adapting the input distance matrix in a pre-processing step, rather than directly integrating the constraints into the clustering algorithm. This makes it possible to try different adaptation strategies, independently of the specific clustering algorithm, and the adapted matrices can be straightforwardly combined with the clustering algorithm of choice. Klein et al. (2002) handle must-link constraints by modifying the input matrix D in the following way: if two instances i and j are linked by a must-link constraint, then the corresponding entry $D_{i,j}$ is set to zero, which forces i and j to be grouped into the same cluster by the underlying clustering algorithm. In addition, distance scores for instances in the neighborhood of i or j are affected: if the distance is reduced for one pair of instances, triangle-inequality may be violated. An all-pairs-shortest-path algorithm propagates must-link constraints to other instances in D that restores triangle inequality.

We use a modified version of this approach. First, as the crowdsourced information may not be completely reliable, the clustering algorithm should be able to override it. We thus do not set $D_{i,j}$ to zero but rather to a small constant value d, that is the smallest non-identity distance value occurring in the matrix. Second, we exploit the

---

[1] This annotation was rather costly, so each scenario was aligned by one annotator only.

inherent transitivity of paraphrase judgments to derive additional constraints: if (i, j) and (j, k) are must links, we assume the pair (i, k) to be a must link as well, and set the distance to d. After the additional constraints are derived, the all-pairs-shortest-path algorithm is applied to the input matrix as in Klein et al. (2002).

We experimented with various state-of-art clustering algorithms including Spectral Clustering and Affinity Propagation (AP). The results presented in section 4 are based on AP, which proved to be most stable and provided the best results.

Determining the number of event-clusters. AP uses a parameter p, which influences the cluster granularity without determining the exact number of clusters beforehand. There is considerable variation between the optimal number of clusters between scenarios, depending on how many event types are required to describe the respective activity patterns (see Section 2). We use an unsupervised method for estimating scenario-specific settings of p, using the mean Silhouette Coefficient (Rousseeuw, 1987). This measure balances optimal inter-cluster tightness and intra-cluster distance, making sure that the elements of each cluster are as similar as possible to each other, and as dissimilar as possible to the elements of all other clusters. We run the unsupervised AP algorithm for each scenario with different settings of p and select the number resulting in the highest total Silhouette Coefficient as the optimal value for p.

3.2 Similarity Features

We now describe how we combine semantic and positional similarity information to obtain the distance measure that captures the similarities between event descriptions.

3.2.1 Semantic Similarity

We inspect different models for word-level similarity, as well as methods of deriving phrase-level semantic similarity from word-level similarity. We use pre-trained Word2Vec (w2v) word vectors (Mikolov et al., 2013) and vector representations (rNN) by Tilk et al. (2016) to obtain word-level similarity information. The rNN vectors are obtained from a neural network trained on large amounts of automatically role-labeled text and capture different aspects of word-level similarity than the w2v representations. We also experimented with WordNet/Lin similarity (Lin, 1998),

but an ablation test (see below) showed that it was not useful.

To derive phrase-level similarity from word-level similarity, we employ the following three different empirically informed methods:

Centroid-based similarity. This method derives a phrase-level vector for an event description by taking the centroid over the word vectors of all content words in the event description. Similarity is computed using cosine.

Alignment-based similarity. Following RKP, we compute a similarity score for a pair of event descriptions by a linear combination of (a) the similarity of the head verbs of the two event descriptions and (b) the total score of the alignments between all noun phrases in the two descriptions, as computed by the Hungarian algorithm (Papadimitriou and Steiglitz, 1982).

Vocabulary similarity. We use the approach in Fernando and Stevenson (2008) to detect paraphrases and calculate semantic similarities between two event descriptions p_1 and p_2 as:

$$sim_{vocab}(\vec{p_1}, \vec{p_2}) = \frac{\vec{p_1} W \vec{p_2}^T}{|\vec{p_1}| \, |\vec{p_2}|} \quad (1)$$

where W is an $n \times n$ matrix that holds the similarities between all the words (vocabulary) in the two event descriptions being compared, n being the length of the vocabulary, and $\vec{p_1}$ and $\vec{p_2}$ are binary vectors representing the presence or absence of the words in the vocabulary.

Combining these three methods with the three word-level similarity measures we obtained a total of 8 different features[2].

3.2.2 Positional Similarity Feature

In addition to the semantic similarity features described above, we also used information about the position in which an event description occurs in an ESD. The basic idea here is that similar event descriptions tend to occur in similar (relative) positions in the ESDs. We set:

$$sim_{pos}(n_1, n_2) = 1 - abs\left(\frac{n_1}{T_1} - \frac{n_2}{T_2}\right) \quad (2)$$

where n_1 and n_2 are the positions of the two event description and T_1 and T_2 represent the total number of event descriptions in the respective ESDs.

---

[2]The *centroid* method can not be combined with Lin similarity.

3.2.3 Combination

We linearly combine our 9 similarity features into a single similarity score, where the weights of the individual features are determined using logistic regression trained (10-fold cross validation) on the paraphrases from the 4 scenarios in the RKP development set (see Section 2). We run an ablation test by considering all possible subsets of features and using the 10 scenarios in the RKP test set, and found that the combination of the following five features performed best:

- centroid-based, alignment-based and vocabulary similarity with w2v vectors

- centroid-based similarity with rNN vectors

- position similarity

3.3 Temporal Script Graphs

After clustering the event descriptions of a given scenario into sets representing the scenario-specific event-types, we build a Temporal Script Graph (TSG) by determining the prototypical order between them. The nodes of the graph are the event types (clusters); an edge from a cluster E to a cluster E' indicates that E typically precedes E'. We induce the edges as follows. We say that an ESD *supports* $E \rightarrow E'$ if there are event descriptions $e \in E$ and $e' \in E'$ such that e precedes e' in the ESD. In a first step, we add an edge $E \rightarrow E'$ to the graph if there are more ESDs that support $E \rightarrow E'$ than $E' \rightarrow E$. In a second step, we compute transitive closure, i.e. we infer an edge $E \rightarrow E'$ in cases where there are clusters E, E', E'' such that $E \rightarrow E''$ and $E'' \rightarrow E'$. Finally, we form "arbitrary order" equivalence classes from those pairs of event clusters which have an equal number of supporting ESDs in either direction and are not yet connected by a directed temporal precedence edge.

This is an extension of the concept of a temporal script graph used in RKP, in order to allow for the flexible event order assumed by our approach. For example, the event descrpitions *preheat the oven* and *mixing ingredients* from the BAKING A CAKE scenario are likely to occur in different clusters, which are members of the same equivalence class, expressing that the event descriptions are not paraphrases, but may occur in any order.

4 Evaluation

4.1 Experimental Setup

We applied different versions of our clustering algorithm to the SMILE+OMICS dataset. In particular, we explored the influence of positional similarity, of the number of seeds (from 0 to 3%), as well as the proportion of the two seed types (outlier vs. stable). As a baseline, we ran the unsupervised clustering algorithm based on semantic similarity only. We evaluated the models on the tasks of event-type induction, paraphrase detection, and temporal order prediction, using the respective gold standard datasets (see Section 2).

Cluster quality. First, we evaluated the quality of the induced event types (i.e. sets of event descriptions) against the SMILE+OMICS gold clusters. We used the B-Cubed metric (Bagga and Baldwin, 1998), which is calculated by averaging per-element precision and recall scores. Amigó et al. (2009) showed B-Cubed to be the metric that appropriately captures all aspects of measuring cluster quality.

Paraphrase detection. For direct comparison with previous work, we tested our model on RKP's binary paraphrase detection task. The model classifies two event descriptions as paraphrases if they end up in the same cluster. We computed standard precision, recall and F-score by checking our classification against the RKP paraphrase dataset.

Temporal order prediction. We tested the quality of the temporal-order relation of the induced TSG structures using the RKP temporal order dataset as follows. For a pair of event descriptions (e, e'), we assume that (1) e precedes e', but not the other way round, if $e \in E$ and $e' \in E'$ for two different clusters E and E' such that $E \rightarrow E'$. (2) e precedes e' *and* vice versa (that is, both event orderings are possible), if $e \in E$ and $e' \in E'$, and E and E' are different clusters, but part of the same equivalence set. In all other cases (i.e. if e and e' are members of the same cluster), we assume that precedence does not hold. We computed standard precision, recall and F-score by checking our classification against the RKP temporal order dataset.

4.2 Results

The main results of our evaluation are shown in Table 1. The last three rows show results for

	Clustering	Paraphrasing			Temporal Ordering		
Model	B-Cubed	Precision	Recall	F-score	Precision	Recall	F-score
Regneri et al. (2010)	–	0.645	**0.833**	0.716	0.658	0.786	0.706
Modi and Titov (2014)	–	–	–	0.645	0.839	**0.843**	**0.841**
Frermann et al. (2014)	–	0.743	0.658	0.689	0.85	0.717	0.776
Baseline: USC	0.525	0.738	0.593	0.646	0.736	0.712	0.722
USC+Position	0.531	0.76	0.623	0.675	0.789	0.766	0.775
SSC+Outlier	0.635	0.781	0.751	0.756	0.858	0.791	**0.822**
SSC+Mixed	**0.655**	**0.796**	0.756	**0.764**	**0.865**	0.784	**0.822**

Table 1: Results on the clustering, paraphrasing and temporal ordering tasks for state-of-the-art models, our unsupervised (USC) and semi-supervised clustering approaches (SSC)

three of our model variants: unsupervised clustering with both semantic and positional information (USC+Position), semi-supervised clustering with positional information and only outlier constraints (3%, SSC+Outlier) and with the best-performing ratio of constraint types (SSC+Mixed, with 2% outliers and 1% stable cases). Row 4 shows the results for our unsupervised clustering baseline with semantic similarity only (USC).

For comparison against previous work, we added the results on the paraphrase and temporal ordering tasks of the MSA model by RKP, the Hierarchical Bayesian model by Frermann et al. (2014) and the Event Embedding model by Modi and Titov (2014) (for details about the latter, see Section 6).

On all three tasks, our best-performing model is SSC with mixed seed data (SSC+Mixed). Our best model outperforms the unsupervised model in RKP by 4.8 points (F-score) on the paraphrasing and by 11.6 points on the temporal ordering task. Interestingly, the performance gain is exclusively due to an increase of precision in both tasks (15.1 and 20.7 points, respectively). Our system comes close, but does not beat Modi and Titov (2014) on their unsupervised state-of-the-art model for temporal ordering, but outperforms it on the paraphrase task by almost 12 points F-score. The use of both positional information and mixed seed data in the distance measure has substantial effects on the quality of the results, improving on the unsupervised clustering baseline and reaching state-of-the-art results.

4.3 Discussion

The largest and most consistent performance gain of our model is due to use of crowdsourced alignment information.

undress
take off all your clothes, take off clothes, take clothes off, remove clothes, get undressed, disrobe, peeloff dresses, remove the clothes, *place clothes in hanger*, take off close, remove clothing, undress, i take off my clothes

adjust temp.
adjust temperature to your liking, wait for hot water, set handle to correct temperature, check the temperature, *adjust the position of shower*, feel for good temperature, adjust water temperature, adjust for desired temperature

soap body
scrub soap over your body, *wash the rest of the body*, repeat soaping body, *wash the body, wet entire body*, wash body with soap, soap body with soap or gel, put bath soap on body, *scrub the body parts*, apply soap, clean body with them, wash body with soap soap body, *add soap to cloth as needed*, i soap up,

dress
put clothes back on, get dressed, apply clothes, put clothes on, put on clothes, dress in clean clothing

Figure 2: Example clusters output by our model for TAKING A SHOWER.

Fig. 2 shows example clusters with script-specific paraphrases captured by our best model for the TAKING A SHOWER scenario. The model was able to capture a wide variety of lexical realizations of undress, including *peel off clothes, disrobe, remove clothes* etc., and similarly for dress, where we get *get dressed, apply clothes, put on clothes*, while these ended up in different clusters in the baseline model (e.g. *get dressed* was clustered together with *shampoo hair* cluster). There are still some incorrect classifications (indicated with italics in Fig. 2); note that these are often near misses rather than blatant errors.

Positional information substantially contributes to the quality of the derived TSGs. While the model using semantic similarity features only put *peel off dresses* in the dress cluster, positional similarity helped placing it correctly in the `undress` cluster, as it appears in the initial segment of its ESD. Positional information sometimes also caused wrong clustering decisions: *place cloth in hanger* typically occurs directly after `undressing`, and thus ended up in the `undress` cluster.

As described above, we collected alignments for outliers and for stable cases and tried several outlier-to-stable ratios. Outliers were much more effective than stable cases, as they improved recall by adjusting cluster boundaries to include scenario-specific functional paraphrases that were semantically dissimilar. Interestingly, adding a small number of stable cases leads to a slight improvement, but adding more stable cases leads to a performance drop, and using only stable cases does not improve the unsupervised baseline at all. Fig. 3 shows how the model improves as more constraints are added.

We tried to reduce the amount of manual annotation in several ways. The decision to derive additional must-links using transitivity paid off: F-score consistently improves by about 1 point F-score. To further increase the set of seeds, we experimented with propagating the links to nearest neighbors of aligned event descriptions, but did not see an improvement. Also, we tried to use alignments obtained by majority vote, which however led to a performance drop, showing that using high quality seeds is crucial.

To make sure that our results are not dependent on the selection of a specific scenario set, we evaluated our model also on the DeScript gold clusters. The results were comparable: B-Cubed improved from 0.551 (RKP: 0.525) to 0.662 (RKP: 0.655). As the DeScript corpus provides 100 ESDs per scenario, we were also able to test whether an increased number of input ESDs also improves clustering performance. We observed no effect with 50 ESDs compared to our model using 25 ESDs, and only a slight (less than 1 point) improvement with the full 100 ESDs dataset.

A leading motivation to use clustering instead of MSA was the opportunity to model flexible event order in script structures. Our expectations were confirmed by the evaluation results. A closer look at the induces TSGs (as shown by the example TSG in Fig. 4), suggests that our system makes extensive use of the option of flexible event ordering.

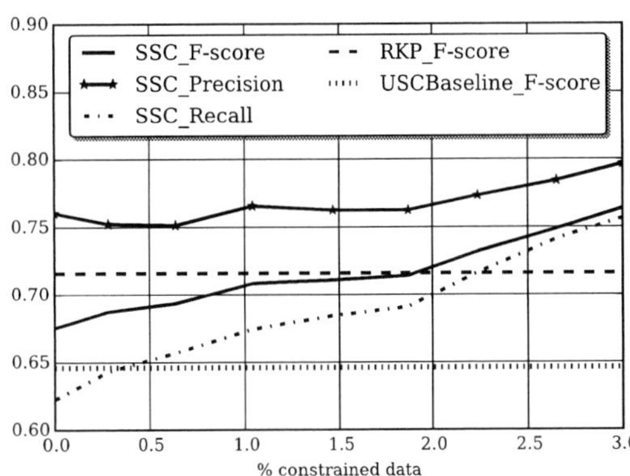

Figure 3: Paraphrase detection results for RKP, for our Unsupervised baseline (USC) and for our best Semi-supervised model (SSC+Mixed)

---

enter bathroom ⇒(turn on shower↔ undress) ⇒(adjust temp.↔ turn off water)⇒get in shower ⇒(soap body↔ close curtains)⇒shampoo hair ⇒(wash hair↔ wash body↔ shave)⇒rinse ⇒exit shower⇒dry off⇒dress

---

Figure 4: Example TSG for TAKING A SHOWER. The arrows stand for default temporal precedence, the parentheses enclose equivalence classes expressing arbitrary temporal order.

5 Costs and Coverage

We have demonstrated that semi-supervised clustering enables the extraction of script knowledge with substantially higher quality than existing methods. But how does the method scale? Can we expect to obtain a script knowledge database with sufficiently wide coverage at reasonable costs?

The process of script extraction requires crowd-sourced data in terms of (1) ESDs and (2) seed alignments. To complete 3%+3% high-quality alignments for the 10 DeScript scenarios via Mechanical Turk (that is, 3% stable cases and 3% outliers), workers spent a total of 37.5 hours, with an average of 3.75 hrs per scenario, ranging from 2.5 (GOING GROCERY SHOPPING) to 7.52 hrs (BAKING A CAKE)[3]. It took on average 2.78 hrs to collect 25 scenario-specific ESDs, that is 6.53 hrs of data acquisition time per scenario.

The costs per scenario are moderate. But how many scenarios must be modeled to achieve suf-

---

[3]We used the DeScript scenarios as reference because they come with equal numbers of ESDs, while the ESD sets in the SMILE+OMICS corpus vary considerably in size.

> *Jessica needs milk.* Jessica wakes up and wants to eat breakfast. She grabs the cereal and pours some into a bowl. She looks in the fridge for milk. There is no milk in the fridge so she can't eat her breakfast. She goes to the store to buy some milk comes home and eats breakfast.
> MAKE BREAKFAST: **C**
>
> GOING GROCERY SHOPPING: **P**

Figure 5: Example ROC-story with scenario annotation.

ficient coverage for the analysis of script knowledge in natural-language texts? Answering this question is not trivial, as scenarios vary considerably in granularity and it is not trivial that the type of script knowledge we model can capture all kinds of event structures, even in narrative texts. In order to provide a rough estimate of coverage for the currently existing script material, we carried out a simple annotation study on the recently published ROC-stories database (Mostafazadeh et al., 2016a). The database consists of 50,000 short narrative texts, collected via Mechanical Turk. Workers were asked to write a 5-sentence length story about an everyday commonsense event, and they were encouraged to write about "anything they have in mind" to guarantee wide distribution across topics.

For our annotation study, we merged the available datasets containing crowdsourced ESD collections (i.e. OMICS, SMILE, and DeScript), excluding two extremely general scenarios (GO OUT-SIDE, CHILDHOOD), which gives us a total of 226 different scenarios.

We randomly selected 500 of the ROC-stories and asked annotators to determine for each story which scenario (if any) was centrally addressed and which scenarios were just referred to or partially addressed with at least one event mention, and to label them with "C" and "P", respectively. See an example story with its annotation in Fig. 5.

Each story was annotated by three students of computational linguistics. To facilitate annotation, the stories were presented alongside ten scenarios whose ESDs showed strongest lexical overlap with the story (calculated as tf-idf). However, annotators were expected to consider the full scenario list[4]. The three annotations were merged us-

ing majority vote. Cases without a clear majority vote containing one single "C" assignment were inspected and adjudicated by the authors of the paper.

26.4% of the stories were judged to centrally refer to one of the scenarios[5]. Although this percentage cannot be directly translated to coverage values, it indicates that the extraction method presented in this paper has the strong potential to provide a script knowledge resource with reasonable costs, which can substantially contribute to the task of text understanding.

6 Related Work

Following the seminal work of Chambers and Jurafsky (2008) and (2009) on the induction of script-like *narrative schemas* from large, unlabeled corpora of news articles, a series of models have been presented for improving the induction method or explore alternative data sources for script learning. Gordon (2010) mined commonsense knowledge from stories describing events in day-to-day life. Jans et al. (2012) studied different ways of selecting event chains and used skipgrams for computing event statistics. Pichotta and Mooney (2014) employed richer event representations, exploiting the interactions between multiple arguments to extract event sequences from a large corpus. Rahimtoroghi et al. (2016) learned contingency relations between events from a corpus of blog posts. All these approaches aim at high recall, resulting in a large amount of wide-coverage, but noisy schemas.

Abend et al. (2015) proposed an edge-factored model to determine the temporal order of events in cooking recipes, but their model is limited to scenarios with an underlying linear order of events. Bosselut et al. (2016) induce prototypical event structure in an unsupervised way from a large collection of photo albums with time-stamped images and captions. This method is however limited by the availability of albums for "special" events such as WEDDING or BARBECUE, in contrast to everyday, trivial activites such as MAKING COFFEE or

---

[4]We are aware that this setup may bias participants toward finding a scenario from our collection, leading to an increase in recall. However, they had the option to label stories where they felt a scenario was only partially addressed in a different way, thus setting these cases apart from those where the scenario was centrally addressed.

[5]While we take the judgment about the "C" class to be quite reliable (24.8% qualified by majority vote, only 1.6 % were added via adjudication), there was considerable confusion about the "P" label. So we decided not to use the "P" label at all.

GOING TO THE DENTIST. Mostafazadeh et al. (2016b) presented the ROC-stories, a dataset of c.a. 50.000 crowdsourced short commonsense everyday story. They propose to use it for the evaluation of script knowledge models, and it may also turn out to be a valuable resource for script learning, although to our knowledge this has not yet been attempted.

Closest to our approach is the work by RKP and subsequent work by Frermann et al. (2014) and Modi and Titov (2014). All these employ the same SMILE+OMICS dataset for evaluation, which we also used to allow for a direct comparison. Frermann et al. (2014) present a Bayesian generative model for joint learning of event types and ordering constraints. Their model promisingly shows that flexible event order in scripts can be suitably modelled. Modi and Titov (2014) focussed mainly on event ordering between script-related predicates, using distributed representations of predicates and arguments induced by a statistical model. They obtained paraphrase sets as a by-product, namely by creating an event timeline and grouping together event mentions corresponding to the same interval.

7 Conclusions

This paper presents a clustering-based approach to inducing script structure from crowdsourced descriptions of scenarios. We use semi-supervised clustering to group individual event descriptions into paraphrase sets representing event types, and induce a temporal order among them. Crowdsourced alignments between event descriptions proved highly effective as seed data. On a paraphrase task, our approach outperforms all previous proposals, while still performing very well on the task of temporal order prediction. A study on the ROC-stories suggests that a model of script knowledge created with our method can cover a large fraction of event structures occurring in topically unrestricted narrative text, thus demonstrating the scalability of our approach.

Acknowledgments

This research was funded by the German Research Foundation (DFG) as part of SFB 1102 'Information Density and Linguistic Encoding'.

References

Omri Abend, Shay B. Cohen, and Mark Steedman. 2015. Lexical event ordering with an edge-factored model. In *Proceedings of the 2015 Conference of the North American Chapter of the Association for Computational Linguistics: Human Language Technologies*, pages 1161–1171, Denver, Colorado, May–June. Association for Computational Linguistics.

Enrique Amigó, Julio Gonzalo, Javier Artiles, and Felisa Verdejo. 2009. A comparison of extrinsic clustering evaluation metrics based on formal constraints. *Information retrieval*, 12(4):461–486.

Amit Bagga and Breck Baldwin. 1998. Algorithms for scoring coreference chains. In *The First International Conference on Language Resources and Evaluation Workshop on Linguistics Coreference*, pages 563–566.

Avron Barr and Edward A. Feigenbaum. 1981. Frames and scripts. In *The Handbook of Artificial Intelligence*, volume 3, pages 216–222. Addison-Wesley, California.

Antoine Bosselut, Jianfu Chen, David Warren, Hannaneh Hajishirzi, and Yejin Choi. 2016. Learning prototypical event structure from photo albums. In *Proceedings of the 54th Annual Meeting of the Association for Computational Linguistics (Volume 1: Long Papers)*, pages 1769–1779, Berlin, Germany, August. Association for Computational Linguistics.

Nathanael Chambers and Dan Jurafsky. 2008. Unsupervised learning of narrative event chains. In *Proceedings of ACL-08: HLT*, pages 789–797, Columbus, Ohio, June. Association for Computational Linguistics.

Nathanael Chambers and Dan Jurafsky. 2009. Unsupervised learning of narrative schemas and their participants. In *Proceedings of the Joint Conference of the 47th Annual Meeting of the ACL and the 4th International Joint Conference on Natural Language Processing of the AFNLP*, pages 602–610, Suntec, Singapore, August. Association for Computational Linguistics.

Richard E. Cullingford. 1977. *Script Application: Computer Understanding of Newspaper Stories*. Ph.D. thesis, Yale University.

Richard Durbin, Sean Eddy, Anders Krogh, and Graeme Mitchison. 1998. *Biological sequence analysis: probabilistic models of proteins and nucleic acids*. Cambridge University Press, Cambridge, UK.

Samuel Fernando and Mark Stevenson. 2008. A semantic similarity approach to paraphrase detection. In *Proceedings of the 11th Annual Research Colloquium of the UK Special Interest Group for Computational Linguistics*.

Lea Frermann, Ivan Titov, and Manfred Pinkal. 2014. A hierarchical bayesian model for unsupervised induction of script knowledge. In *Proceedings of the 14th Conference of the European Chapter of the Association for Computational Linguistics*, pages 49–57, Gothenburg, Sweden, April. Association for Computational Linguistics.

Andrew S. Gordon. 2010. Mining commonsense knowledge from personal stories in internet weblogs. In *Proceedings of the First Workshop on Automated Knowledge Base Construction*, Grenoble, France.

Rakesh Gupta and Mykel J. Kochenderfer. 2004. Common sense data acquisition for indoor mobile robots. In *Proceedings of the 19th National Conference on Artificial intelligence*, pages 605–610. AAAI Press.

Hannaneh Hajishirzi and Erik T. Mueller. 2012. Question answering in natural language narratives using symbolic probabilistic reasoning. In *Proceedings of the Twenty-Fifth International Florida Artificial Intelligence Research Society Conference*, pages 38–43.

Bram Jans, Steven Bethard, Ivan Vulić, and Marie-Francine Moens. 2012. Skip N-grams and ranking functions for predicting script events. In *Proceedings of the 13th Conference of the European Chapter of the Association for Computational Linguistics*, pages 336–344, Avignon, France, April. Association for Computational Linguistics.

Dan Klein, Sepandar D. Kamvar, and Christopher D. Manning. 2002. From instance-level constraints to space-level constraints: Making the most of prior knowledge in data clustering. In *Proceedings of the Nineteenth International Conference on Machine Learning*, pages 307–314.

Dekang Lin. 1998. An information-theoretic definition of similarity. In *In Proceedings of the 15th International Conference on Machine Learning*, pages 296–304.

Tomas Mikolov, Kai Chen, Greg S. Corrado, and Jeffrey Dean. 2013. Efficient estimation of word representations in vector space. In *Proceedings of the International Conference on Learning Representations*.

Ashutosh Modi and Ivan Titov. 2014. Inducing neural models of script knowledge. In *Proceedings of the Eighteenth Conference on Computational Natural Language Learning*, pages 49–57, Ann Arbor, Michigan, June. Association for Computational Linguistics.

Nasrin Mostafazadeh, Nathanael Chambers, Xiaodong He, Devi Parikh, Dhruv Batra, Lucy Vanderwende, Pushmeet Kohli, and James Allen. 2016a. A corpus and cloze evaluation for deeper understanding of commonsense stories. In *Proceedings of the 2016 Conference of the North American Chapter of the Association for Computational Linguistics: Human Language Technologies*, pages 839–849, San Diego, California, June. Association for Computational Linguistics.

Nasrin Mostafazadeh, Lucy Vanderwende, Wen-tau Yih, Pushmeet Kohli, and James Allen. 2016b. Story cloze evaluator: Vector space representation evaluation by predicting what happens next. In *Proceedings of the 1st Workshop on Evaluating Vector Space Representations for NLP*, pages 24–29.

Erik T. Mueller. 2004. Understanding script-based stories using commonsense reasoning. *Cognitive Systems Research*, 5(4):307–340.

Christos H. Papadimitriou and Kenneth Steiglitz. 1982. *Combinatorial Optimization: Algorithm und Complexity*. Dover Publications, Mineola, NY.

Karl Pichotta and Raymond Mooney. 2014. Statistical script learning with multi-argument events. In *Proceedings of the 14th Conference of the European Chapter of the Association for Computational Linguistics*, pages 220–229, Gothenburg, Sweden, April. Association for Computational Linguistics.

Elahe Rahimtoroghi, Ernesto Hernandez, and Marilyn Walker. 2016. Learning fine-grained knowledge about contingent relations between everyday events. In *Proceedings of the 17th Annual Meeting of the Special Interest Group on Discourse and Dialogue*, pages 350–359.

Altaf Rahman and Vincent Ng. 2011. Narrowing the modeling gap: a cluster-ranking approach to coreference resolution. *Journal of Artificial Intelligence Research*, 40:469–521.

Lisa F. Rau, Paul S. Jacobs, and Uri Zernik. 1989. Information extraction and text summarization using linguistic knowledge acquisition. *Information Processing & Management*, 25(4):419–428.

Michaela Regneri, Alexander Koller, and Manfred Pinkal. 2010. Learning script knowledge with web experiments. In *Proceedings of the 48th Annual Meeting of the Association for Computational Linguistics*, pages 979–988, Uppsala, Sweden, July. Association for Computational Linguistics.

Peter J. Rousseeuw. 1987. Silhouettes: A graphical aid to the interpretation and validation of cluster analysis. *Journal of Computational and Applied Mathematics*, 20:53 – 65.

Roger C. Schank and Robert P. Abelson. 1977. *Scripts, Plans, Goals, and Understanding: An Inquiry into Human Knowledge Structures*. Erlbaum, Hillsdale, NJ.

Ottokar Tilk, Vera Demberg, Asad Sayeed, Dietrich Klakow, and Stefan Thater. 2016. Event participant modelling with neural networks. In *Proceedings of the 2016 Conference on Empirical Methods in Natural Language Processing*, pages 171–182, Austin, Texas, November. Association for Computational Linguistics.

Lilian D. A. Wanzare, Alessandra Zarcone, Stefan Thater, and Manfred Pinkal. 2016. A crowd-sourced database of event sequence descriptions for the acquisition of high-quality script knowledge. In N. Calzolari (Conference Chair), K. Choukri, T. Declerck, S. Goggi, M. Grobelnik, B. Maegaard, J. Mariani, H. Mazo, A. Moreno, J. Odijk, and S. Piperidis, editors, *Proceedings of the Tenth International Conference on Language Resources and Evaluation (LREC 2016)*. European Language Resources Association (ELRA).

A Consolidated Open Knowledge Representation for Multiple Texts

Rachel Wities[* 1]**, Vered Shwartz**[1]**, Gabriel Stanovsky**[1]**, Meni Adler**[1]**, Ori Shapira**[1]**,
Shyam Upadhyay[2]**, Dan Roth**[2]**, Eugenio Martinez Camara**[3]**, Iryna Gurevych**[3,4] **and
Ido Dagan**[1]

[1]Bar-Ilan University, Ramat-Gan, Israel
[2]University of Illinois at Urbana-Champaign, IL, USA
[3]Ubiquitous Knowledge Processing Lab (UKP), Technische Universitat Darmstadt
[4]Ubiquitous Knowledge Processing Lab (UKP-DIPF),
German Institute for Educational Research

```
{rachelvov,vered1986,gabriel.satanovsky,meni.adler,obspp18}@gmail.com
{upadhya3,danr}@illinois.edu, {camara,gurevych}@ukp.informatik.tu-darmstadt.de
                          dagan@cs.biu.ac.il
```


Abstract

We propose to move from Open Information Extraction (OIE) ahead to Open Knowledge Representation (OKR), aiming to represent information conveyed jointly in a set of texts in an open text-based manner. We do so by consolidating OIE extractions using entity and predicate coreference, while modeling information containment between coreferring elements via lexical entailment. We suggest that generating OKR structures can be a useful step in the NLP pipeline, to give semantic applications an easy handle on consolidated information across multiple texts.

1 Introduction

Natural language understanding involves identifying, classifying, and integrating information about events and other propositions mentioned in text. While much effort has been invested in generic methods for analyzing single sentences and detecting the propositions they contain, little thought and effort has been put into the integration step: how to systematically consolidate and represent information contributed by propositions originating from multiple texts. Consolidating such information, which is typically both complementary and partly overlapping, is needed to construct multi-document summaries, to combine evidence when answering questions that cannot be answered based on a single sentence, and to populate a knowledge base while relying on multiple pieces of evidence (see Figure 1 for a motivating

example). Yet, the burden of integrating information across multiple texts is currently delegated to downstream applications, leading to various partial solutions in different application domains.

This paper suggests that a common consolidation step and a corresponding knowledge representation should be part of the "standard" semantic processing pipeline, to be shared by downstream applications. Specifically, we pursue an Open Knowledge Representation (OKR) framework that captures the information expressed jointly in multiple texts while relying solely on the terminology appearing in those texts, without requiring pre-defined external knowledge resources or schemata.

As we focus in this work on investigating an *open* representation paradigm, our proposal follows and extends the Open Information Extraction (OIE) approach. We do that by first extracting textual predicate-argument tuples, each corresponding to an individual proposition mention. We then merge these mentions by accounting for proposition coreference, an extended notion of event coreference. This process yields consolidated propositions, each corresponding to a single fact, or assertion, in the described scenario. Similarly, entity coreference links are used to establish reference to real-world entities. Taken together, our proposed representation encodes information about events and entities in the real world, similarly to what is expected from structured knowledge representations. Yet, being an open text-based representation, we record the various lexical terms used to describe the scenario. Further, we model information redundancy and containment among these terms through lexical entailment.

In this paper we specify our proposed represen-

---

*Corresponding author

Proceedings of the 2nd Workshop on Linking Models of Lexical, Sentential and Discourse-level Semantics, pages 12–24,
Valencia, Spain, April 3, 2017. ©2017 Association for Computational Linguistics

1. Turkey **forces down** Syrian plane.	4. Turkish PM says plane was carrying ammunition for Syria government.
2. Damascus sends note to Ankara over Syrian plane.	5. Last night Turkish F16s **grounded** a Syrian passenger jet.
3. Turkey Escalates Confrontation with Syria.	6. Russia angry at Turkey about Russian passengers.

Figure 1: A sample of news headlines, illustrating the need for information consolidation. Two mentions of the same proposition, for which event coreference holds, are highlighted, with the predicate in bold and the arguments underlined. Some information is redundant, but may be described at different granularity levels; for example, different mentions describe the interception target as a *plane* and as a *jet*, where *jet* entails *plane* and is accordingly more informative.

tation, while specifying the involved annotation sub-tasks from which our structures are composed. We then describe our annotated dataset, of news headline tweets about 27 news stories, which is the first to be jointly annotated for all our required sub-tasks. We also provide initial predicted baseline results for each of the sub-tasks, pointing at the limitations of current state of the art.[1]

Overall, our main contribution is in proposing to create a consolidated representation for the information contained in multiple texts, and in specifying how such representation can be created based on entity and event coreference and lexical entailment. An accompanying contribution is our annotated dataset, which can be used to analyze the involved phenomena and their interactions, and as a development and test set for automated generation of OKR structures. We further note that while this paper focuses on creating an *open* representation, by consolidating Open IE propositions, future work may investigate the consolidation of other semantic sentence representations, for example AMR (Abstract Meaning Representation) (Banarescu et al., 2013), while exploiting similar principles to those proposed here.

2 Background: Relevant Component Tasks

In this section we describe the prior annotation tasks on which we rely in our representation, as described later in Section 3.

2.1 Open Information Extraction

Open IE (Open Information Extraction) (Etzioni et al., 2008) is the task of extracting coherent propositions from a sentence, each comprising a relation phrase and two or more argument phrases. For example, *(plane, **landed in**, Ankara).*

Open IE has gained substantial and consistent attention, and many automatic extractors were cre-

ated (e.g., Fader et al. (2011); Del Corro and Gemulla (2013)). Open IE's extractions were also shown to be effective as intermediate sentence-level representation in various downstream applications (Stanovsky et al., 2015; Angeli et al., 2015). Analogously, we conjecture a similar utility of our OKR structures at the multi-text level.

Open IE does not assign roles to the arguments associated with each predicate, as in other single-sentence representations like SRL (Semantic Role Labeling) (Carreras and Màrquez, 2005; Palmer et al., 2010). While the former is not consistent in assigning argument slots to the same arguments across different propositions, the latter requires predefined thematic role ontologies. A middle ground was introduced by QA-SRL (He et al., 2015), where predicate-argument structures are represented using question-answer pairs, e.g. (what landed somewhere?, *plane*), (where did something land?, *Ankara*).

2.2 Coreference Resolution Tasks

In our representation, we use coreference resolution to consolidate mentions of the same entity or the same event across multiple texts.

Entity Coreference Entity coreference resolution identifies mentions in a text that refer to the same real-world entity (Soon et al., 2001; Ng and Cardie, 2002; Bengtson and Roth, 2008; Clark and Manning, 2015; Peng et al., 2015). In the cross-document variant, Cross Document Coreference Resolution (CDCR), mentions of the same entity can also appear in multiple documents in a corpus (Singh et al., 2011).

Event Coreference Event coreference determines whether two event descriptions (mentions) refer to the same event (Humphreys et al., 1997). Cross document event coreference (CDEC) is a variant of the task in which mentions may occur in different documents (Bagga and Baldwin, 1999).

Compared to within document event coreference (Chen et al., 2009; Araki et al., 2014; Liu et

---

[1] Our dataset, detailed annotation guidelines, the annotation tool and the baseline implementations are available at `https://github.com/vered1986/OKR`.

al., 2014; Peng et al., 2016), the problem of cross document event coreference has been relatively under-explored (Bagga and Baldwin, 1999; Bejan and Harabagiu, 2014). Standard benchmarks for this task are the Event Coreference Bank (ECB) (Bejan and Harabagiu, 2008) and its extensions, that also annotate entity coreference: EECB (Lee et al., 2012) and ECB+ (Cybulska and Vossen, 2014). See (Upadhyay et al., 2016) for more details on cross document event coreference.

Differently from our dataset described in Section 4, ECB and its extensions do not establish predicate-argument annotations. A secondary line of work deals with aligning predicates across document pairs, as done in Roth and Frank (2012). PARMA (Wolfe et al., 2013) treated the task as a token-alignment problem, aligning also arguments, while Wolfe et al. (2015) added joint constraints to align predicates and their arguments.

Using Coreference for Consolidation Recognizing that two elements are corefering can help in consolidating textual information. In discourse representation theory (DRT), a proposition applies to all co-referring entities (Kamp et al., 2011). In recognizing textual entailment (Dagan et al., 2013), lexical substitution of co-referring elements is useful (Stern and Dagan, 2012). For example, in Figure 1, sentence (1) together with the coreference relation between *plane* and *jet* entail that "Turkey forces down Syrian jet."

2.3 Lexical Inference

Recognizing lexical inferences is an important component in semantic tasks, in order to bridge lexical variability in texts. For instance, in text summarization, lexical inference can help identifying redundancy, when two candidate sentences for the summary differ only in terms that hold a lexical inference relation (e.g. "the plane landed in *Ankara*" and "the plane landed in *Turkey*"). Recognizing the inference direction, e.g. that *Ankara* is more specific than *Turkey*, can help in selecting the desired granularity level of the description.

There has been consistent attention to recognizing lexical inference between terms. Some methods aim to recognize a general lexical inference relation (e.g. (Kotlerman et al., 2010; Turney and Mohammad, 2015)), others focus on a specific semantic relation, mostly hypernymy (Hearst, 1992; Snow et al., 2005; Santus et al., 2014; Shwartz et al., 2016), while recent methods classify a pair of

terms to a specific semantic relation out of several (Baroni et al., 2012; Weeds et al., 2014; Pavlick et al., 2015; Shwartz and Dagan, 2016). It is worth noting that most existing methods are indifferent to the context in which the target terms occur, with the exception of few works, which were mostly focused on a narrow aspect of lexical inference, e.g. lexical substitution (Melamud et al., 2015).

Determining entailment between predicates is a different sub-task, which has also been broadly explored (Lin and Pantel, 2001; Duclaye et al., 2002; Szpektor et al., 2004; Schoenmackers et al., 2010; Roth and Frank, 2012). Berant et al. (2010) achieved state-of-the-art results on the task by constructing a predicate entailment graph optimizing a global objective function. However, performance should be further improved in order to be used accurately within semantic applications.

3 Proposed Representation

Our Open Knowledge Representation (OKR) aims to capture the consolidated information expressed jointly in a set of texts. In some analogy to structured knowledge bases, we would like the elements of our representation to correspond to entities in the described scenario and to statements (propositions) that relate them. Still, in the spirit of Open IE, we would like the representation to be open, while relying only on the natural language terminology in the given texts without referring to predefined external knowledge.

This section specifies our proposed structure, with a running example in Figure 2. The specification involves two aspects: the first is defining the component annotation sub-tasks involved in creating our representation, following those reviewed in Section 2; the second is specifying how we derive from these component annotations a consolidated representation. These two aspects are interleaved along the presentation, where for each step we first describe the relevant annotations and then how we use them to create the corresponding component of the representation.

3.1 Entities

To represent entities, we first annotate the text by entity mentions and coreference. Following the typical notion for these tasks, an *entity mention* corresponds to a word or multi-word expression that refers to an object or concept in the described scenario (in the broader sense of "entity"). Ac-

Original texts:

(1) Turkey forces down Syrian plane.

(2) Syrian jet grounded by Turkey carried munitions from Moscow.

(3) Intercepted Syrian plane carried ammunition from Russia.

Entities:

E_1 = {*Turkey*}, E_2 = {*Syrian*}, E_3 = {*plane, jet*}

E_4 = {*munitions, ammunition*}, E_5 = {*Moscow*}, E_6 = {*Russia*}

Proposition Mentions (+ coreference + argument alignment):

P_1: [a_1] **forces down** [a_2] (*Turkey* [E_1], *plane* [E_3])

P_2: [a_1] [a_2] (*Syrian* [E_2], *plane* [E_3]) (implicit)

P_2: [a_1] [a_2] (*Syrian* [E_2], *jet* [E_3]) (implicit)

P_1: [a_2] **grounded by** [a_1] (*jet* [E_3], *Turkey* [E_1])

P_3: [a_1] **carried** [a_2] **from** [a_3]
(*jet* [E_3], *munitions* [E_4], *Moscow* [E_5])

P_1: **intercepted** [a_2] (*jet* [E_3])

P_2: [a_1] [a_2] (*Syrian* [E_2], *plane* [E_3]) (implicit)

P_3: [a_1] **carried** [a_2] **from** [a_3]
(*plane* [E_3], *ammunition* [E_6], *Russia* [E_6])

Consolidated Propositions:

P_1 : { [a_1] **forces down** [a_2]; [a_2] **grounded by** [a_1]; **intercepted** [a_2] }   [a_1: {E_1}, a_2: {E_3}]

P_2: { [a_1] [a_2] (implicit) }   [a_1: {E_2}, a_2: {E_3}]

P_3: { [a_1] **carried** [a_2] **from** [a_3] }   [a_1: {E_3}, a_2: {E_4}, a_3: {E_5, E_6}]

Entailment Graphs:

Propositions: P_1 :
[a_1] **forces down** [a_2] ⟷ [a_2] **grounded by** [a_1]
intercepted [a_2]

Entities:
E_3: **jet** ⟶ **plane**
E_4: **ammunition** ⟶ **munitions**

Arguments: $P_3.a_3$: **Moscow** ⟶ **Russia**

(a)

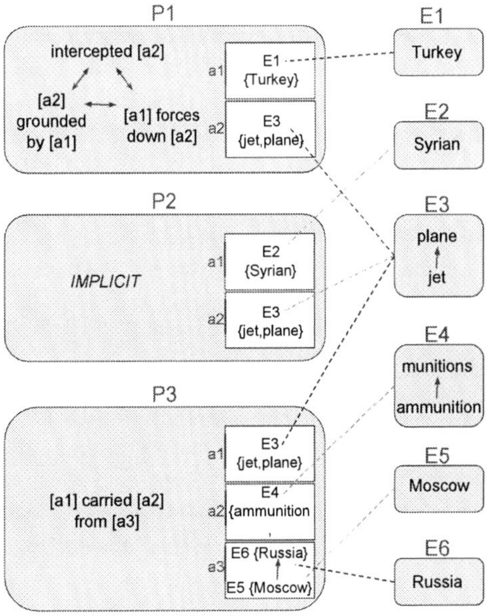

(b)

Figure 2: An illustration of our OKR formalism **(a)**, with a corresponding graphical view of the consolidated structure **(b)**. In (b), dashed lines connect entities to their instantiation within arguments, while allowing graph-traversal inferences such as: what is the relation between *Turkey* and *Russia*? *Turkey* intercepted a plane that carried ammunition from *Russia* (the path from E_1 to E_6 via the darker dashed lines).

cordingly, we represent an *entity* in the described scenario by the coreference cluster of all its mentions. We represent the coreferring cluster of mentions by the multiset of its terms, keeping pointers to each term's mentions (see Entities in Figure 2; to avoid clutter, pointers are not presented in the figure). We note that we take an inclusive view which regards concepts as entities, for example the adjective *Syrian* is considered an entity mention that may corefer with *Syria*.

3.2 Proposition Mentions and Consolidated Propositions

To represent propositions, we first annotate Open IE style extractions, which we term *proposition mentions*. Each mention consists of a predicate expression, e.g. around verbs or nominalizations, and a set of arguments (see Proposition Mentions in Figure 2). We deviate slightly from standard Open IE formats by representing the predicate expression as a template, with place holders for the arguments (marked with brackets in the figure). This follows the common representation of predicates within predicate inference rules, as in DIRT (Lin and Pantel, 2001), and allows the span of entity arguments to correspond exactly to the entity term. Further, as typical in Open IE, modalities and negations become part of the lexical elements of the predicate. Notice that at this stage an argument mention is already associated with its corresponding entity. Further, we annotate implicit predicates when a predication between two entities is implied, without an explicit predicate expression, as common for noun modifications (P_2

in the figure). Nested propositions are represented by having one proposition mention as an argument of the other (e.g. "the [plane] **was forced to** [land in Ankara]").

To link different mentions of the same real world fact, we annotate *proposition coreference*, which generalizes the notion of event coreference to cover all types of predications (e.g., *John is Mary's brother* would co-refer with *Mary is John's sister*). This annotation specifies the coreference relation for a cluster of proposition mentions (denoted by the same proposition index P_i in Figure 2), as well as an alignment of their arguments, (denoted by matching argument indexes within the same proposition cluster). We then consider a *proposition* to correspond to a coreference cluster of proposition mentions, which jointly describe the referred real-world fact.

Yet, a cluster of co-referring proposition mentions does not provide a succinct representation for the aggregated textual description of a proposition. To that end, we aggregate the information in the cluster into a *Consolidated Proposition*, composed of a *consolidated predicate* and *consolidated arguments*. Similar to entity representation, a consolidated predicate is represented by the set of all predicate expressions appearing in the cluster. A consolidated argument is specified by the set of all entities (or propositions, in case of having one proposition being an argument of another one) that occupy this argument's slot in the different mentions. As with entities, each element in this representation is accompanied by a set of pointers to all its original mentions (omitted from the figure). A graphical illustration of this structure is given in Figure 2(b) (for now, ignore the arrows within some of the nodes).

A consolidated proposition encodes compactly all possible textual descriptions for the referred proposition, which can be generated from its mentions taken jointly. Each description can be generated by picking one possible predicate expression and then picking one possible lexical choice for each argument. For example, P_1 may be described as *Turkey intercepted a plane*, *Turkey forces down a jet* etc. Some of these descriptions correspond to original mentions in the text, while others can be induced through coreference (as reviewed at the end of Section 2.2). The representation of a consolidated proposition thus does not depend on the particular way in which lexical choices were split across the different proposition mentions.

3.3 Lexical Entailment Graphs

The set of descriptions encoded in a consolidated proposition is highly redundant. To make it more useful, we would like to model the information overlap between different lexical choices. For example, we want to know that *Turkey intercepted a plane* is more general than, or equivalently, is entailed by, *Turkey intercepted a jet*. To that end, we annotate the lexical entailment relations between the elements in each component of our representation, that is, within each consolidated predicate, consolidated argument and entity. This yields a *lexical entailment graph* within each component (see figure 2), which models the information containment relationships between different descriptions.

Notice that in our setting the lexical entailment relation is considered within the given context (see Section 2.3). For example, *grounded* and *forced down* may not be generically synonymous, but they do convey equivalent information in a given context of forcing a flying plane to land. Contradictions are modeled to a limited extent, by annotating contradiction relations (in context) between elements of our entailment graphs, for example when different figures are reported for the number of casualties in a disaster. This is a natural representation, since contradiction is often modeled within a three-way entailment classification task. Modeling of broader cases of contradiction is left for future work.

The entailment graphs yield better modeling of the supporting text mentions (and their total count) for each possible description. For example, knowing that *Moscow* entails *Russia*, we can assume in P_3 two supporting mentions for knowing that the ammunition was carried from Russia, while having only one supporting mention for the more detailed information regarding Moscow being the origin. Such frequency support often correlates with confidence and prominence of information, which, together with generality modeling, may be very useful in applications such as multi-document summarization or question answering. Finally, the graphical view of our representation lends itself to graph-based inferences, such as looking for all connections between two entities, similar to aggregated inferences over structured knowledge graphs (see example in Figure 2(b)).

# Entities	1262
# Entity mentions	5074
# Entity singeltons	777
# Propositions	1406
# Proposition mentions	4311
# Proposition Singletons	949
Avg. mentions per entity chain	8.86
Avg. distinct lemmas per entity chain	2.00
Avg. mentions per proposition chain	7.35
Avg. distinct lemmas per prop. chain	2.24
Avg. number of elements per arg. chain	1.08

Table 2: Twitter dataset statistics. Distinct lemma terms per proposition chain were calculated only on explicit propositions. Average number of elements per argument chain measures how many distinct entities or propositions were part of the same argument.

In summary, our open knowledge representation consists of the following: *entities*, generated by detecting entity mentions and coreference; *consolidated propositions*, composed of consolidated predicates and arguments, which are generated by detecting proposition mentions and coreference relations between them; *lexical entailment graphs* for entities, consolidated predicates and consolidated arguments, which specify the inference relations between the elements within each of these components. This yields a compact representation of all possible descriptions of the statements jointly asserted by the set of texts, as induced via coreference-based inference, while tracking information containment between different descriptions as well as tracking their (induced) supporting mentions.

4 News-Related Tweets Dataset

Following the formal definition of our OKR structures, we compiled a corpus with gold annotations of our 5 subtasks (listed in Table 1). As outlined in the previous section, our structures follow deterministically from these annotations. Specifically, we make use of the news-related tweets collected in the Twitter Event Detection Dataset (McMinn et al., 2013), which clusters tweets from major news networks and other sources discussing the same event (for example, the grounding of a Syrian plane by the Turkish government). We chose to annotate news related tweets in this first dataset for several reasons: (1) they represent self contained assertions, (2) they tend to be relatively factual and succinct, and (3) by looking at several news sources we can obtain a corpus with high redundancy, which our representation aims to address.

We note that while this dataset exhibits a limited amount of linguistic complexity, making it suitable for a first investigation, it still represents a very practical use case of consolidating information in a large stream of tweets about a news story.

This annotation serves two main purposes. First, it validates the feasibility of our annotation scheme in terms of annotator requirements, training and agreement. Second, to the best of our knowledge, this is the first time these core NLP annotations are annotated *in parallel* over the same texts. Following, this annotation has the potential of becoming a useful resource spurring future research into *joint prediction* of these annotations. For instance, predicate argument structures may benefit from co-reference signals, and entity extraction systems may exploit signals from lexical entailment.

Overall, we annotated 1257 tweets from 27 clusters. We release the dataset both in full OKR format, as well as ECB-like "light" format, containing only the annotated co-reference chains. Overall corpus statistics are depicted in Table 2.

4.1 Dataset Characteristics

An analysis of the annotations reveals interesting and unique characteristics of our annotated corpus.

First, the part of speech distribution of entities and predicates (Table 3) shows that our corpus captures information beyond the current focus on verb-centric applications and corpora in NLP. Namely, our corpus contains a vast number of nonverbal predications (67%), and a relatively large number of adjectival entities, owing to the fact that our structure annotates concepts such as "northern" or "Syrian" as entities in an implicit relation.

Second, the average number of unique lemmas per entity and proposition chains (2.00 and 2.24, respectively) shows that our corpus exhibits a fair amount of non-trivial lexical variability.

Finally, roughly 96% of our entailment graphs (entity and proposition) form a connected component. This data provides an interesting potential for investigating and modeling lexical inference relations within coreference chains.

4.2 Annotation Procedure and Agreement

The annotation was performed by two native English speakers with linguistic academic background, which had 10 hours of in house training. The entire annotation process took 200 person-hours using a graphical tool purposely-designed

| Task | Entity Ment. | Entity Co-reference | | | | Prop. Mentions | | Proposition Co-Reference | | | | | | | | Entailment | |
| | | | | | | Pred. | Arg. | Predicate | | | | Argument | | | | Entity | Prop |
	avg. acc	MUC	B^3	CEAF	CoNLL F_1	avg. acc	avg. acc	MUC	B^3	CEAF	CoNLL F_1	MUC	B^3	CEAF	CoNLL F_1	F_1	F_1
IAA	.85	.87	.92	.92	.90	.74 (.93, .72)†	.85	.86	.88	.76	.83	.99	.99	.98	.99	.70	.82
Pred	.58	.84	.89	.81	.85	.41 (.73, .25)†	.37	.47	.67	.56	.56	.93	.97	.94	.95	.44	.56

Table 1: Inter-Annotator Agreement (top) and off-the-shelf state-of-the-art predicted performance (bottom, see Section 5) for the OKR subtasks: (1) Entity mention extraction (for prediction we use F1 score) (2) Entity co-reference (3) Proposition Extraction (predicate identification and argument detection) (4) Proposition Co-reference (predicate coreference and argument alignment), and (5) Entailment graphs (entity and proposition entailment; argument entailment figures are not presented due to very low statistics). † Numbers in parenthesis denote verbal vs. non-verbal predicates, respectively.

to facilitate the incremental annotation for all subtasks . We employ the QA-SRL annotation methodology to help determining Open IE predicate and argument spans in the gold standard, for its intuitiveness for non-expert annotators (He et al., 2015). Five clusters were annotated independently by both annotators and were used to measure their agreement on the task. The other clusters were annotated by one annotator and reviewed by an expert.

We measure agreement separately on each annotation subtask. After each task in our pipeline we keep only the consensual annotations. For example, we measure entity coreference agreement only for entity mentions that were annotated by both annotators. For entity, predicate and argument mention agreement, we average the accuracy of the two annotators, each computed while taking the other as a gold reference.

For entity, predicate, and argument co-reference we calculated coreference resolution metrics: the link-based MUC (Vilain et al., 1995), the mention-based B^3 (Bagga and Baldwin, 1998), the entity-based CEAF, and the widely adopted CoNLL F_1 measure which is an average of the three. For entity and proposition entailment we compute the F_1 score over the annotated directed edges in each entailment graph, as is common for entailment agreement metrics (Berant et al., 2010).

We macro-averaged these scores to obtain an overall agreement on the 5 events annotated by both annotators. The agreement scores for the two annotators are shown in Table 1, and overall show high levels of agreement. A qualitative analysis of the more common disagreements between annotators is shown in Table 4.

Overall, this shows that our parallel annotation is indeed feasible; agreement on each of the subtasks is relatively high and on par with reported inter-annotator agreement on similar tasks.

POS	Nouns	Verbs	Adj's	Impl.	Others
Ent. Dist.	.85	.01	.09	–	.05
Pred. Dist.	.40	.33	.04	.18	.04

Table 3: Entity and Predicate distribution across part of speech tags: nouns, verbs, adjectives, non-lexicalized (implicit) and all others.

Disagreement Type	Examples
Phrasal verbs	$[placed\ to\ leave]_{pred.}$ **vs.** $[placed\ to]_{pred.} [leave]_{pred.}$ $[faces\ charges]_{pred.}$ **vs.** $[faces]_{pred.} [charges]_{arg.}$
Nominalizations	$[suspect]_{ent.}\ plane$ **vs.** $[suspect]_{pred.}\ plane$ $[terror]_{ent.}\ attack$ **vs.** $[terror]_{pred.}\ attack$ $U.S.\ [elections]_{ent.}$ **vs.** $U.S.\ [elections]_{pred.}$
Entailment	$fuel{\rightarrow}gas$ **vs.** $gas{\rightarrow}fuel$ $scandal{\rightarrow}case$ **vs.** $case{\rightarrow}scandal$

Table 4: Typical cases of annotator disagreements. Annotated spans are denoted by square brackets, subscript denotes label for the mention (predicate, argument or entity).

5 Baselines

As we have shown in previous sections, our structure is derived from known "core" NLP tasks, extended where needed to fit our consolidated representation. Subsequently, a readily available means of automatically recovering OKR is through a pipeline which uses off-the-shelf models for each of the subtasks.

To that end, we employ publicly available tools and simple baselines which approximate the current state-of-the-art in each of these subtasks. For brevity sake, in the rest of the section we briefly describe each of these baselines. For a more detailed technical description see the OKR repository (https://github.com/vered1986/OKR).

For *Entity Mention* extraction we use the spaCy NER model[2] in addition to annotating all of the nouns and adjectives as entities. For *Proposition Mention* detection we use Open IE propositions extracted from PropS (Stanovsky et al., 2016), where non-restrictive arguments were reduced following Stanovsky and Dagan (2016). For *Proposi-

---

[2]https://spacy.io/

tion and *Entity coreference*, we clustered the entity mentions based on simple lexical similarity metrics (e.g., lemma matching and Levenshtein distance), shown to be effective on our news tweets.[3]

For *Argument Mention* detection we attach the components (entities and propositions) as arguments of predicates when the components are syntactically dependent on them. *Argument Co-reference* is simply predicted by marking co-reference if and only if the arguments are both mentions of the same entity co-reference chain. For *Entity Entailment* purposes we used knowledge resources (Shwartz et al., 2015) and a pre-trained model for HypeNET (Shwartz et al., 2016) to obtain a score for all pairs of Wikipedia common words (unigrams, bigrams, and trigrams). A threshold for the binary entailment decision was then calibrated on a held out development set. Finally, for *Predicate Entailment* we used the entailment rules extracted by Berant et al. (2012).

5.1 Results and Error Analysis

Using the same metrics used for measuring inter-annotator agreement, we evaluated how well the presented models were able to recover the different facets of the OKR gold annotations. The performance on the different subtasks is presented in Table 1 (bottom).

We measure the performance of each component separately, while taking the annotations for all previous steps from the gold human annotations. This allows us to examine the performance of the current component, alleviating any incurred errors from previous steps. Thus, we can identify technological "bottle-necks" – the steps which most significantly lower predicted OKR accuracy using current off-the-shelf tools.

First, we noticed that non-verbal predicates pose a challenge for current verb-centric systems. This primarily manifests in low scores for identifying entities, predicates and arguments. Many entity mention errors are due to nominalizations mistakenly annotated as entities. When excluding gold nominalizations, the entity mention baseline F1 score rises from 0.58 to 0.63. As mentioned

earlier (Section 4.2) nominalizations were also one of the main challenges for the annotators. Furthermore, recognizing nominalizations and other non-verbal predicates, which are very common in our dataset (see Table 3), proves to be a difficult task. Indeed, we see a significant improvement in performance when comparing verbal predicate mention performance to non-verbal performance (accuracy of 0.73 vs. 0.25). Finally, argument identification was hard mainly because of inconsistencies in verbal versus nominal predicate-argument structure in dependency trees.[4]

The low performance in predicate coreference compared to entity coreference can be explained by the higher variability of predicate terms. The argument co-reference task becomes easy given gold predicate-argument structures, as most arguments are singletons (i.e. composed of a single element).

Finally, while the performance of the predicate entailment component reflects the current state-of-the-art (Berant et al., 2012; Han and Sun, 2016), the performance on entity entailment is much worse than the current state-of-the-art in this task as measured on common lexical inference test sets. We conjecture that this stems from the nature of the entities in our dataset, consisting of both named entities and common nouns, many of which are multi-word expressions, whereas most work in entity entailment is focused on single word common nouns. Furthermore, it is worth noting that our annotations are of naturally occurring texts, and represent lexical entailment in real world co-reference chains, as opposed to synthetically compiled test sets which are often used for this task.

While several tasks achieve reasonable performance on our datasets, most tasks leave room for improvement. These bottle-necks are bound to hinder the performance of a pipeline end-to-end system. Future research into OKR should first target these areas; either as a pipeline or in a joint learning framework.

6 Applications and Related Work

The need to consolidate information originating from multiple texts is common in applications that summarize multiple text into some structure, such as multi-document summarization and knowledge-base population. Currently, there is no

---

[3] We chose simple metrics over complex state-of-the-art entity coreference models since they target different scenarios from ours: first, they focus on named entities, and are likely to overlook common nouns like *plane* and *jet*. Second, since we work in the context of the same news story, it is reasonable to assume that, for example, two mentions of a person with the same last name belong to the same entity.

[4] E.g., "Facebook's acquisition of Instagram" is represented differently than "Facebook acquired Instagram".

systematic solution, and the burden of integrating information across multiple texts is delegated to downstream applications, leading to partial solutions which are geared to specific applications.

Multi-Document Summarization (MDS) (Barzilay et al., 1999) is a task whose goal is to produce a concise summary from a set of related text documents, such that it includes the most important information in a non-redundant manner. While extractive summarization selects salient sentences from the document collection, abstractive summarization generates new sentences, and is considered a more promising yet more difficult task.

A recent approach for abstractive summarization generates a graphical representation of the input documents by: (1) parsing each sentence/document into a meaning representation structure; and (2) merging the structures into a single structure that represents the entire summary, e.g. by identifying coreferring items.

In that sense, this approach is similar to OKR. However, current methods applying this approach are still limited. Gerani et al. (2014) parse each document to discourse tree representation (Joty et al., 2013), aggregating them based on entity coreference. Yet, they work with a limited set of (discourse) relations, and rely on coreference only between entities, which was detected manually.

Similarly, Liu et al. (2015) parse each input sentence into an individual AMR graph (Banarescu et al., 2013), and merge those into a single graph through identical concepts. This work extends the AMR formalism of canonicalized representation per entity or event to multiple sentences. However, they only focus on certain types of named entities, and collapse two entities based on their names rather than on coreference.

Event-Centric Knowledge Graphs (ECKG) (Vossen et al., 2016; Rospocher et al., 2016) is another related work which represent news articles as graphs. Event nodes are linked to DBPedia (Auer et al., 2007), with the goal of enriching entities and events with dynamic knowledge. For example, an event describing the interception of the Syrian plane by Turkey will be linked in DBPedia to *Syria* and *Turkey*.

We propose that OKR can help the described applications by providing a general underlying representation for multiple texts, obviating the need to develop specialized consolidation methods for each application. We can expect the use of OKR structures in MDS to shift the research efforts in this task to other components, e.g. generation, and eventually contribute to improving state of the art on this task. Similarly, an algorithm creating the ECKG structure can benefit from building upon a consolidated structure such as OKR, rather than working directly on free text.

7 Conclusions

In this paper we advocate the development of representation frameworks for the consolidated information expressed in a set of texts. The key ingredients of our approach are the extraction of proposition structures which capture individual statements and their merging based on entity and event coreference. Coreference clusters are proposed as a handle on real world entities and facts, while still being self-contained within the textual realm. Lexical entailment is proposed to model information containment between different textual descriptions of the same real world components.

While we developed an "open" KR framework, future work may investigate the creation of similar models based on structures that do refer to external resources (such as PropBank, as in Abstract Meaning Representation – AMR). Gradually, fine grained semantic phenomena may be addressed, such as factuality, attribution and modeling sub-events and cross-event relationships. Finally, we plan to investigate performing the core annotation sub-tasks via crowdsourcing, for scalability.

Acknowledgments

This work was supported in part by grants from the MAGNET program of the Israeli Office of the Chief Scientist (OCS) and the German Research Foundation through the German-Israeli Project Cooperation (DIP, grant DA 1600/1-1), and by Contract HR0011-15-2-0025 with the US Defense Advanced Research Projects Agency (DARPA).

References

Gabor Angeli, Melvin Jose Johnson Premkumar, and Christopher D. Manning. 2015. Leveraging linguistic structure for open domain information extraction. In *Proceedings of the 53rd Annual Meeting of the Association for Computational Linguistics and the 7th International Joint Conference on Natural Language Processing (Volume 1: Long Papers)*, pages

344–354, Beijing, China, July. Association for Computational Linguistics.

Jun Araki, Zhengzhong Liu, Eduard Hovy, and Teruko Mitamura. 2014. Detecting subevent structure for event coreference resolution. In *Proceedings of the Ninth International Conference on Language Resources and Evaluation (LREC-2014)*, pages 4553–4558, Reykjavik, Iceland. European Language Resources Association (ELRA).

Sören Auer, Christian Bizer, Georgi Kobilarov, Jens Lehmann, Richard Cyganiak, and Zachary Ives. 2007. The semantic web. In *Lecture Notes in Computer Science*, volume 4825, chapter Dbpedia: A nucleus for a web of open data, pages 722–735. Springer Berlin Heidelberg.

Amit Bagga and Breck Baldwin. 1998. Algorithms for scoring coreference chains. In *Proceedings of the First International Conference on Language Resources and Evaluation (LREC'98)*, volume 1, pages 563–566, Granada, Spain. European Language Resources Association (ELRA).

Amit Bagga and Breck Baldwin. 1999. Cross-document event coreference: Annotations, experiments, and observations. In *Proceedings of the Workshop on Coreference and its Applications*, pages 1–8, College Park, Maryland,US. Association for Computational Linguistics.

Laura Banarescu, Claire Bonial, Shu Cai, Madalina Georgescu, Kira Griffitt, Ulf Hermjakob, Kevin Knight, Philipp Koehn, Martha Palmer, and Nathan Schneider. 2013. Abstract meaning representation for sembanking. In *Proceedings of the 7th Linguistic Annotation Workshop and Interoperability with Discourse*, pages 178–186, Sofia, Bulgaria, August. Association for Computational Linguistics.

Marco Baroni, Raffaella Bernardi, Ngoc-Quynh Do, and Chung-chieh Shan. 2012. Entailment above the word level in distributional semantics. In *Proceedings of the 13th Conference of the European Chapter of the Association for Computational Linguistics*, pages 23–32, Avignon, France, April. Association for Computational Linguistics.

Regina Barzilay, Kathleen R. McKeown, and Michael Elhadad. 1999. Information fusion in the context of multi-document summarization. In *Proceedings of the 37th Annual Meeting of the Association for Computational Linguistics*, pages 550–557, College Park, Maryland, USA, June. Association for Computational Linguistics.

Cosmin Bejan and Sanda Harabagiu. 2008. A linguistic resource for discovering event structures and resolving event coreference. In *Proceedings of the Sixth International Conference on Language Resources and Evaluation (LREC'08)*, pages 2881–2887, Marrakech, Morocco, May. European Language Resources Association (ELRA).

Cosmin A. Bejan and Sanda Harabagiu. 2014. Unsupervised event coreference resolution. *Computational Linguistics*, 40(2):311–347.

Eric Bengtson and Dan Roth. 2008. Understanding the value of features for coreference resolution. In *Proceedings of the 2008 Conference on Empirical Methods in Natural Language Processing*, pages 294–303, Honolulu, Hawaii. Association for Computational Linguistics.

Jonathan Berant, Ido Dagan, and Jacob Goldberger. 2010. Global learning of focused entailment graphs. In *Proceedings of the 48th Annual Meeting of the Association for Computational Linguistics*, pages 1220–1229, Uppsala, Sweden, July. Association for Computational Linguistics.

Jonathan Berant, Ido Dagan, and Jacob Goldberger. 2012. Learning entailment relations by global graph structure optimization. *Computational Linguistics*, 38(1):73–111.

Xavier Carreras and Lluís Màrquez. 2005. Introduction to the CoNLL-2005 shared task: Semantic role labeling. In *Proceedings of the Ninth Conference on Computational Natural Language Learning (CoNLL-2005)*, pages 152–164, Ann Arbor, Michigan, June. Association for Computational Linguistics.

Zheng Chen, Heng Ji, and Robert Haralick. 2009. A pairwise event coreference model, feature impact and evaluation for event coreference resolution. In *Proceedings of the Workshop on Events in Emerging Text Types*, pages 17–22, Borovets, Bulgaria, September. Association for Computational Linguistics.

Kevin Clark and Christopher D. Manning. 2015. Entity-centric coreference resolution with model stacking. In *Proceedings of the 53rd Annual Meeting of the Association for Computational Linguistics and the 7th International Joint Conference on Natural Language Processing (Volume 1: Long Papers)*, pages 1405–1415, Beijing, China, July. Association for Computational Linguistics.

Agata Cybulska and Piek Vossen. 2014. Using a sledgehammer to crack a nut? lexical diversity and event coreference resolution. In *Proceedings of the Ninth International Conference on Language Resources and Evaluation (LREC-2014)*, pages 4545–4552, Reykjavik, Iceland. European Language Resources Association (ELRA).

Ido Dagan, Dan Roth, and Mark Sammons. 2013. *Recognizing textual entailment*. Morgan & Claypool Publishers, San Rafael, CA.

Luciano Del Corro and Rainer Gemulla. 2013. Clausie: Clause-based open information extraction. In *Proceedings of the 22Nd International Conference on World Wide Web*, WWW '13, pages 355–366, Rio de Janeiro, Brazil. Association for Computing Machinery.

Florence Duclaye, François Yvon, and Olivier Collin. 2002. Using the web as a linguistic resource for learning reformulations automatically. In *Proceedings of the Third International Conference on Language Resources and Evaluation (LREC'02)*, volume 2, pages 390–396, Las Palmas, Canary Islands - Spain. European Language Resources Association (ELRA).

Oren Etzioni, Michele Banko, Stephen Soderland, and Daniel S. Weld. 2008. Open information extraction from the web. *Communications of the ACM*, 51(12):68–74, December.

Anthony Fader, Stephen Soderland, and Oren Etzioni. 2011. Identifying relations for open information extraction. In *Proceedings of the 2011 Conference on Empirical Methods in Natural Language Processing*, pages 1535–1545, Edinburgh, Scotland, UK., July. Association for Computational Linguistics.

Shima Gerani, Yashar Mehdad, Giuseppe Carenini, Raymond T. Ng, and Bita Nejat. 2014. Abstractive summarization of product reviews using discourse structure. In *Proceedings of the 2014 Conference on Empirical Methods in Natural Language Processing (EMNLP)*, pages 1602–1613, Doha, Qatar, October. Association for Computational Linguistics.

Xianpei Han and Le Sun. 2016. Context-sensitive inference rule discovery: A graph-based method. In *Proceedings of COLING 2016, the 26th International Conference on Computational Linguistics: Technical Papers*, pages 2902–2911, Osaka, Japan, December. The COLING 2016 Organizing Committee.

Luheng He, Mike Lewis, and Luke Zettlemoyer. 2015. Question-answer driven semantic role labeling: Using natural language to annotate natural language. In *Proceedings of the 2015 Conference on Empirical Methods in Natural Language Processing*, pages 643–653, Lisbon, Portugal, September. Association for Computational Linguistics.

Marti A. Hearst. 1992. Automatic acquisition of hyponyms from large text corpora. In *COLING 1992 Volume 2: Proceedings of the 15th International Conference on Computational Linguistics*, volume 2, pages 539–545. Association for Computational Linguistics.

Kevin Humphreys, Robert Gaizauskas, and Saliha Azzam. 1997. Event coreference for information extraction. In *Proceedings of a Workshop on Operational Factors in Practical, Robust Anaphora Resolution for Unrestricted Texts*, pages 75–81, Madrid, Spain, July. Association for Computational Linguistics.

Shafiq Joty, Giuseppe Carenini, Raymond Ng, and Yashar Mehdad. 2013. Combining intra- and multi-sentential rhetorical parsing for document-level discourse analysis. In *Proceedings of the 51st Annual Meeting of the Association for Computational Linguistics (Volume 1: Long Papers)*, pages 486–496,

Sofia, Bulgaria, August. Association for Computational Linguistics.

Hans Kamp, Josef Van Genabith, and Uwe Reyle. 2011. Discourse representation theory. In *Handbook of philosophical logic*, volume 15, pages 125–394. Springer Netherlands.

Lili Kotlerman, Ido Dagan, Idan Szpektor, and Maayan Zhitomirsky-Geffet. 2010. Directional distributional similarity for lexical inference. *Natural Language Engineering*, 16(04):359–389.

Heeyoung Lee, Marta Recasens, Angel Chang, Mihai Surdeanu, and Dan Jurafsky. 2012. Joint entity and event coreference resolution across documents. In *Proceedings of the 2012 Joint Conference on Empirical Methods in Natural Language Processing and Computational Natural Language Learning*, pages 489–500, Jeju Island, Korea, July. Association for Computational Linguistics.

Dekang Lin and Patrick Pantel. 2001. Dirt - discovery of inference rules from text. In *Proceedings of the Seventh ACM SIGKDD International Conference on Knowledge Discovery and Data Mining*, KDD '01, pages 323–328, San Francisco, California. Association for Computing Machinery.

Zhengzhong Liu, Jun Araki, Eduard Hovy, and Teruko Mitamura. 2014. Supervised within-document event coreference using information propagation. In *Proceedings of the Ninth International Conference on Language Resources and Evaluation (LREC-2014)*, pages 4539–4544, Reykjavik, Iceland. European Language Resources Association (ELRA).

Fei Liu, Jeffrey Flanigan, Sam Thomson, Norman Sadeh, and Noah A. Smith. 2015. Toward abstractive summarization using semantic representations. In *Proceedings of the 2015 Conference of the North American Chapter of the Association for Computational Linguistics: Human Language Technologies*, pages 1077–1086, Denver, Colorado, May–June. Association for Computational Linguistics.

Andrew J. McMinn, Yashar Moshfeghi, and Joemon M. Jose. 2013. Building a large-scale corpus for evaluating event detection on twitter. In *Proceedings of the 22Nd ACM International Conference on Information & Knowledge Management*, CIKM '13, pages 409–418, San Francisco, California, USA. Association for Computing Machinery.

Oren Melamud, Ido Dagan, and Jacob Goldberger. 2015. Modeling word meaning in context with substitute vectors. In *Proceedings of the 2015 Conference of the North American Chapter of the Association for Computational Linguistics: Human Language Technologies*, pages 472–482, Denver, Colorado, May–June. Association for Computational Linguistics.

Vincent Ng and Claire Cardie. 2002. Improving machine learning approaches to coreference resolution.

In *Proceedings of 40th Annual Meeting of the Association for Computational Linguistics*, pages 104–111, Philadelphia, Pennsylvania, USA, July. Association for Computational Linguistics.

Martha Palmer, Daniel Gildea, and Nianwen Xue. 2010. Semantic role labeling. *Synthesis Lectures on Human Language Technologies*, 3(1):1–103.

Ellie Pavlick, Johan Bos, Malvina Nissim, Charley Beller, Benjamin Van Durme, and Chris Callison-Burch. 2015. Adding semantics to data-driven paraphrasing. In *Proceedings of the 53rd Annual Meeting of the Association for Computational Linguistics and the 7th International Joint Conference on Natural Language Processing (Volume 1: Long Papers)*, pages 1512–1522, Beijing, China, July. Association for Computational Linguistics.

Haoruo Peng, Kai-Wei Chang, and Dan Roth. 2015. A joint framework for coreference resolution and mention head detection. In *Proceedings of the Nineteenth Conference on Computational Natural Language Learning*, pages 12–21, Beijing, China, July. Association for Computational Linguistics.

Haoruo Peng, Yangqiu Song, and Dan Roth. 2016. Event detection and co-reference with minimal supervision. In *Proceedings of the 2016 Conference on Empirical Methods in Natural Language Processing*, pages 392–402, Austin, Texas, November. Association for Computational Linguistics.

Marco Rospocher, Marieke van Erp, Piek Vossen, Antske Fokkens, Itziar Aldabe, German Rigau, Aitor Soroa, Thomas Ploeger, and Tessel Bogaard. 2016. Building event-centric knowledge graphs from news. *Web Semantics: Science, Services and Agents on the World Wide Web*, 37:132–151.

Michael Roth and Anette Frank. 2012. Aligning predicate argument structures in monolingual comparable texts: A new corpus for a new task. In **SEM 2012: The First Joint Conference on Lexical and Computational Semantics – Volume 1: Proceedings of the main conference and the shared task, and Volume 2: Proceedings of the Sixth International Workshop on Semantic Evaluation (SemEval 2012)*, pages 218–227, Montréal, Canada, 7-8 June. Association for Computational Linguistics.

Enrico Santus, Alessandro Lenci, Qin Lu, and Sabine Schulte im Walde. 2014. Chasing hypernyms in vector spaces with entropy. In *Proceedings of the 14th Conference of the European Chapter of the Association for Computational Linguistics, volume 2: Short Papers*, pages 38–42, Gothenburg, Sweden, April. Association for Computational Linguistics.

Stefan Schoenmackers, Jesse Davis, Oren Etzioni, and Daniel Weld. 2010. Learning first-order horn clauses from web text. In *Proceedings of the 2010 Conference on Empirical Methods in Natural Language Processing*, pages 1088–1098, Cambridge, MA, October. Association for Computational Linguistics.

Vered Shwartz and Ido Dagan. 2016. Path-based vs. distributional information in recognizing lexical semantic relations. In *Proceedings of the 5th Workshop on Cognitive Aspects of the Lexicon (CogALex - V)*, pages 24–29, Osaka, Japan, December. The COLING 2016 Organizing Committee.

Vered Shwartz, Omer Levy, Ido Dagan, and Jacob Goldberger. 2015. Learning to exploit structured resources for lexical inference. In *Proceedings of the Nineteenth Conference on Computational Natural Language Learning*, pages 175–184, Beijing, China, July. Association for Computational Linguistics.

Vered Shwartz, Yoav Goldberg, and Ido Dagan. 2016. Improving hypernymy detection with an integrated path-based and distributional method. In *Proceedings of the 54th Annual Meeting of the Association for Computational Linguistics (Volume 1: Long Papers)*, pages 2389–2398, Berlin, Germany, August. Association for Computational Linguistics.

Sameer Singh, Amarnag Subramanya, Fernando Pereira, and Andrew McCallum. 2011. Large-scale cross-document coreference using distributed inference and hierarchical models. In *Proceedings of the 49th Annual Meeting of the Association for Computational Linguistics: Human Language Technologies*, pages 793–803, Portland, Oregon, USA, June. Association for Computational Linguistics.

Rion Snow, Daniel Jurafsky, and Andrew Y. Ng. 2005. Learning syntactic patterns for automatic hypernym discovery. In *Advances in Neural Information Processing Systems*, volume 17, pages 1297–1304. MIT Press.

Wee M. Soon, Hwee T. Ng, and Daniel C. Y. Lim. 2001. A machine learning approach to coreference resolution of noun phrases. *Computational linguistics*, 27(4):521–544.

Gabriel Stanovsky and Ido Dagan. 2016. Annotating and predicting non-restrictive noun phrase modifications. In *Proceedings of the 54th Annual Meeting of the Association for Computational Linguistics (Volume 1: Long Papers)*, pages 1256–1265, Berlin, Germany, August. Association for Computational Linguistics.

Gabriel Stanovsky, Ido Dagan, and Mausam. 2015. Open IE as an intermediate structure for semantic tasks. In *Proceedings of the 53rd Annual Meeting of the Association for Computational Linguistics and the 7th International Joint Conference on Natural Language Processing (Volume 2: Short Papers)*, pages 303–308, Beijing, China, July. Association for Computational Linguistics.

Gabriel Stanovsky, Jessica Ficler, Ido Dagan, and Yoav Goldberg. 2016. Getting more out of syntax with props. *arXiv preprint*.

Asher Stern and Ido Dagan. 2012. Biutee: A modular open-source system for recognizing textual entailment. In *Proceedings of the ACL 2012 System Demonstrations*, pages 73–78, Jeju Island, Korea, July. Association for Computational Linguistics.

Idan Szpektor, Hristo Tanev, Ido Dagan, and Bonaventura Coppola. 2004. Scaling web-based acquisition of entailment relations. In Dekang Lin and Dekai Wu, editors, *Proceedings of EMNLP 2004*, pages 41–48, Barcelona, Spain, July. Association for Computational Linguistics.

Peter D. Turney and Saif M. Mohammad. 2015. Experiments with three approaches to recognizing lexical entailment. *Natural Language Engineering*, 21(03):437–476.

Shyam Upadhyay, Nitish Gupta, Christos Christodoulopoulos, and Dan Roth. 2016. Revisiting the evaluation for cross document event coreference. In *Proceedings of COLING 2016, the 26th International Conference on Computational Linguistics*.

Marc Vilain, John Burger, John Aberdeen, Dennis Connolly, and Lynette Hirschman. 1995. A model-theoretic coreference scoring scheme. In *Proceedings of the 6th conference on Message understanding*, pages 45–52, Columbia, Maryland. Association for Computational Linguistics.

Piek Vossen, Rodrigo Agerri, Itziar Aldabe, Agata Cybulska, Marieke van Erp, Antske Fokkens, Egoitz Laparra, Anne-Lyse Minard, Alessio Palmero Aprosio, German Rigau, et al. 2016. Newsreader: Using knowledge resources in a cross-lingual reading machine to generate more knowledge from massive streams of news. *Knowledge-Based Systems*, 110:60–85.

Julie Weeds, Daoud Clarke, Jeremy Reffin, David Weir, and Bill Keller. 2014. Learning to distinguish hypernyms and co-hyponyms. In *Proceedings of COLING 2014, the 25th International Conference on Computational Linguistics: Technical Papers*, pages 2249–2259, Dublin, Ireland, August. Dublin City University and Association for Computational Linguistics.

Travis Wolfe, Benjamin Van Durme, Mark Dredze, Nicholas Andrews, Charley Beller, Chris Callison-Burch, Jay DeYoung, Justin Snyder, Jonathan Weese, Tan Xu, and Xuchen Yao. 2013. Parma: A predicate argument aligner. In *Proceedings of the 51st Annual Meeting of the Association for Computational Linguistics (Volume 2: Short Papers)*, pages 63–68, Sofia, Bulgaria, August. Association for Computational Linguistics.

Travis Wolfe, Mark Dredze, and Benjamin Van Durme. 2015. Predicate argument alignment using a global coherence model. In *Proceedings of the 2015 Conference of the North American Chapter of the Association for Computational Linguistics: Human Language Technologies*, pages 11–20, Denver, Colorado, May–June. Association for Computational Linguistics.

Event-Related Features in Feedforward Neural Networks Contribute to Identifying Causal Relations in Discourse

Edoardo Maria Ponti
LTL, University of Cambridge
ep490@cam.ac.uk

Anna Korhonen
LTL, University of Cambridge
alk23@cam.ac.uk

Abstract

Causal relations play a key role in information extraction and reasoning. Most of the times, their expression is ambiguous or implicit, i.e. without signals in the text. This makes their identification challenging. We aim to improve their identification by implementing a Feedforward Neural Network with a novel set of features for this task. In particular, these are based on the position of event mentions and the semantics of events and participants. The resulting classifier outperforms strong baselines on two datasets (the Penn Discourse Treebank and the CSTNews corpus) annotated with different schemes and containing examples in two languages, English and Portuguese. This result demonstrates the importance of events for identifying discourse relations.

1 Introduction

The identification of causal and temporal relations is potentially useful to many NLP tasks (Mirza et al., 2014), such as information extraction from narrative texts (e.g., question answering, text summarization, decision support) and reasoning through inference based on a knowledge source (Ovchinnikova et al., 2010).

A number of resources provide examples of causal relations annotated between event mentions (Mirza et al., 2014) or text spans (Bethard et al., 2008). Among the second group, there are corpora compliant with the assumptions of the Rhetorical Structure Theory (RST) in various languages (Carlson et al., 2002; Aleixo and Pardo, 2008), and the Penn Discourse Treebank (Prasad et al., 2007). The latter counts the largest amount of ex-

amples and is the only resource distinguishing between explicit and implicit relations.

The discourse signal marking causal relations is often ambiguous (i.e. shared with other kinds of relation), or lacking altogether. Identifying implicit causal relations is challenging for several reasons. They often entail a temporal relation of precedence, but this condition is not mandatory (Bethard et al., 2008; Mirza et al., 2014). Moreover, implicit causal relations are partly subjective and have low inter-annotator agreement (Grivaz, 2012; Dunietz et al., 2015). Finally, they have to be detected through linguistic context and world knowledge: unfortunately, this information cannot be approximated by explicit relations deprived of their signal (Sporleder and Lascarides, 2008). Notwithstanding the partial redundancy between signal and context, implicit examples and explicit examples belonging to the same class appear to be too dissimilar linguistically.

Although various techniques have been proposed for the task, ranging from distributional metrics (Riaz and Girju, 2013, *inter alia*) to traditional machine learning algorithms (Lin et al., 2014, *inter alia*), few have been based on deep learning. Those that have used deep learning have mostly relied on lexical features (Zhang et al., 2015; Zhang and Wang, 2015). The aim of our work is to enrich Artificial Neural Networks with features that capture insights from linguistic theory (§ 2) as well as related works (§ 3). In particular, they capture information about the content and position of the events involved in the relation. After presenting the datasets (§ 4), the method (§ 6) and the experimental results (§ 7) we conclude (§ 8) by highlighting that the observed improvements stem from the link between event semantics and discourse relations. Although our work focuses on implicit causal relations, the proposed features are shown to be beneficial also for explicit instances.

Proceedings of the 2nd Workshop on Linking Models of Lexical, Sentential and Discourse-level Semantics, pages 25–30,
Valencia, Spain, April 3, 2017. ©2017 Association for Computational Linguistics

2 Events in Linguistic Theory

Events are complex entities bridging between semantic meaning and the syntactic form (Croft, 2002). The token expressing an event in a text is called a mention and usually consists in a verbal predicate. An event denotes a situation and consists of various components, such as participants and aspect. Participants are entities taking part in the situation, each playing a specific semantic role (Fillmore, 1968; Dowty, 1991). Aspect is the structure of the situation over time and is partly inherent to verbs (Vendler, 1967).

Within discourse, events can establish between themselves different kinds of relation, among which a causal relation (Pustejovsky et al., 2003). This relation is asymmetrical, bridging between a cause and an effect. Discourse-level causation is expressed explicitly through verbs (e.g. *to cause* or *to enable*) (Wolff, 2007) or adverbial markers, either inter-clausal (e.g. *because*) or inter-sentential (e.g. *indeed*). These markers are often ambiguous. Moreover, causation is not necessarily explicit: it can be entailed by the speakers and inferred by the listeners only through world knowledge (Grivaz, 2012).

Both explicit and implicit relations are regulated by a long-standing cognitive principle, namely diagrammatical iconicity. According to this principle the tightness of the morphosyntactic packaging of two expressions is proportional to the degree of semantic integration of the concepts they denote (Haiman, 1985). The relevance of this principle for causal relations has been validated empirically by comparing constructions used to describe causation in visual stimuli (Kita et al., 2010): such constructions were affected by the mediation of an animate participant and the absence of spatial contact or temporal contiguity.

This principle is useful to distinguish causality from other relations. Among adverbial clauses, those expressing cause preserve more independence from the main (effect) clause than the others cross-linguistically. Independence is measured by the freedom in their relative order, the autonomous intonation contour, and non-reduced grammatical categories or valence of verbs (Lakoff, 1984; Diessel and Hetterle, 2011; Cristofaro, 2005). The iconicity principle predicts that this morphosyntactic behaviour corresponds to situations not necessarily sharing time, place and participants from a semantic point of view.

3 Previous Work

Many previous works identified causal relations using metrics or traditional machine learning algorithms. Metrics of the 'causal potential' of event pairs were estimated using distributional information (Beamer and Girju, 2009), verb pairs (Riaz and Girju, 2013) or discourse relation markers (Do et al., 2011). Other techniques employed manually defined rules, consisting in high-level patterns (Grivaz, 2012) or a set of axioms (Ovchinnikova et al., 2010).

The machine learning approaches formulated causal relation identification as a binary classification problem. This problem sometimes involved an intermediate step of discourse marker prediction (Zhou et al., 2010). Features based on fine-grained syntactic representations proved particularly helpful (Wang et al., 2010), and were sometimes supplemented with information about word polarity, verb classes, and discourse context (Pitler et al., 2009; Lin et al., 2014).

Few approaches based on deep learning have been proposed for discourse relation classification so far. Zhang et al. (2015) focused on implicit relations. They introduced a Shallow Convolutional Neural Network that learns exclusively from lexical features. It adopts some strategies to amend the sparseness and imbalance of the dataset, such as a shallow architecture, naive convolutional operations, random under-sampling, and normalization. This approach outperforms baselines based on a Support Vector Machine, a Transductive Support Vector Machine, and a Recursive AutoEncoder.

Moreover, related work on nominal relation classification (Zeng et al., 2014; Zhang and Wang, 2015) showed improvements due to using additional features (neighbours and hypernyms of nouns), as well as measuring the relative distance of each token in a sentence from the target nouns. Although these features are possibly relevant for the identification of causal relations, they have not been investigated for this task before.

4 Datasets

We ran our experiment on two datasets representing different annotation schemes and different languages: the Penn Discourse Treebank in English (Prasad et al., 2007) and the CSTNews corpus in Brazilian Portuguese (Aleixo and Pardo, 2008). The Penn Discourse Treebank was chosen because it distinguishes between explicit and implicit rela-

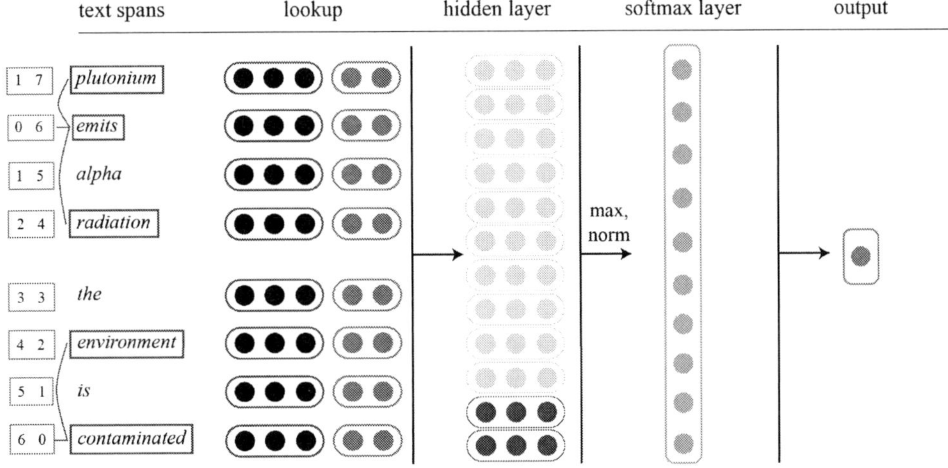

Figure 1: Layers of the Feedforward Neural Network with enriched features.

tions and offers the widest set of examples. Relations are classified into four categories at the coarse-grained level: *Contingency* is considered as the positive class, whereas the others as the negative class.[1] We divided the corpus into a training set (sections 2-20), a validation set (sections 0-1), and a test set (sections 21-22), following Pitler et al. (2009) and Zhang et al. (2015).

On the other hand, he CSTNews corpus contains documents in Brazilian Portuguese annotated according to the Rhetorical Structure Theory. We filtered the texts to keep only relations among leaves in the discourse tree (i.e. containing text spans). The examples labelled as *volitional-cause*, *non-volitional-cause result*, and *purpose* were assigned to the positive class and the others to the negative class. In this case, no distinction was available between implicit and explicit relations. The data partitions in the datasets are detailed in Table 1.

Set	PDTB	CSTNews
Training	3342/9290	190/1101
Validation	295/888	19/143
Test	279/767	19/142

Table 1: Number of examples: positive/negative

5 Features

The most basic kind of features we fed to our algorithm is lexical features, i.e. the vectors stemming from the look-up of the words in every sentence. Vectors are obtained from a model trained with *gensim* (Řehůřek and Sojka, 2010) on Wikipedia. Moreover, we included some additional features: event-related and positional features.

In order to obtain these, the PDTB and CSTNews corpora were parsed using MATE tools (Bohnet, 2010). This parser was trained on the English and Portuguese treebanks available in the Universal Dependency collection (Nivre et al., 2016). In particular, for each of the two related sentences we employed the syntactic trees to discover its root (considered as the event mention) and the nominal modifiers of the root (considered as the participants).[2] We extracted the vector representations of their lemmas, which we call event-related features. Moreover, we assigned to each token two integers representing its absolute linear distance from either event mention. These are called positional features.

The combination of lexical and additional features is called enriched feature set, as opposed to a basic feature set with just lexical features. As an example, consider Figure 1. The lemmas of the two roots are *emit* and *contaminate*. Those of their

---

[1] *Contingency* overlaps with the fine-grained category *Cause* for implicit relations: *Condition* instead can be hardly conveyed without an explicit hypothetical marker (e.g. *if*).

[2] The syntactic root is often, but not necessarily, a verb. Its nominal modifiers are dependent nouns labelled as subject, direct object, or indirect object.

nominal dependents are *plutonium+radiation* and *environment*, respectively. Moreover, the token *alpha*, for instance, is assigned the integers 1 (distance from *emits*) and 5 (distance from *contaminated*).

The rationale of the additional features is that similar features were employed successfully for nominal relation classification (Zeng et al., 2014). Moreover, they are motivated linguistically. Positional features encode the distance and hence the iconic principle, whereas event-related features account for the semantics of the event and its participants (see § 2).

6 Method

We describe here the architecture of the Feedforward Neural Network with an enriched feature set. The core components of the architecture are a look-up step, a hidden layer and the final logistic regression layer where a softmax estimates the probabilities of the two classes. These are are shown in Figure 1. Positional features are concatenated to the input after the look-up step, and are represented as grey nodes. Event-related features instead are concatenated to the output of the hidden layer, and are represented as blue nodes. The training set was under-sampled randomly: positive examples were pruned in order to obtain the same amount of negative and positive examples.[3] Afterwards, all the sentences of the training set were padded with zeroes to equalize them to a length n. Each word was transformed into its corresponding D-dimensional vector by looking up a word embedding matrix E. This matrix is a parameter of the model and is initialized with pre-trained vectors. Afterwards, each vector was concatenated along the D-dimensional axis with its two neighbouring vectors and its two positional features.

This input representation x was then fed to the hidden layer. It underwent a non-linear transformation with a weight and a bias as parameters, and the hyperbolic tangent *tanh* as activation function. The weight is a matrix $W_1 \in \mathbb{R}^{D \times h}$, where h is an hyper-parameter defining the size of the hidden layer. The bias, on the other hand, is a vector $b_1 \in \mathbb{R}^h$. Both were initialised by uniformly sampling values from the symmetric interval suggested by Glorot and Bengio (2010). The output

of this transformation was concatenated with four word embeddings of the two events and the two (max-pooled) sets of their participants. The resulting matrix underwent a max pooling operation over the n axis, which yielded a vector.

Finally, the output of the hidden layer was fed into a Logistic Regression layer. As above, it was multiplied to a weight $W_2 \in \mathbb{R}^{h \times 2}$ and added to a bias $b_2 \in \mathbb{R}^2$. Note that the shape of these parameters along a dimension has length 2 because this is the number of classes to output. Contrary to the hidden layer, both parameters were initialized as zeros. The output of Logistic Regression was squashed by a softmax function σ, which yielded the probability for each class given the example.

The set of parameters of the algorithm is $\theta = \{E, W_1, b_1, W_2, b_2\}$. The loss function is based on binary cross-entropy and is regularised by the squared norm of the parameters scaled by a hyperparameter ℓ. Given an input array of indices to the embedding matrix x_i, the event-related features x_e, the positional features x_p, and a true class y, the objective function is as shown in Equation 1:

$$J = -\sum_{x,y} \sigma(W_2 || \max_n (tanh(W_1 \cdot (x_i \cdot E \oplus x_e) +$$
$$+ b_1) \oplus x_p)|| + b_2) \log P(y) + \ell ||\theta||^2. \quad (1)$$

The optimization of the objective function was performed through mini-batch stochastic gradient descent, running for 150 epochs. Early stopping was enforced to avoid over-fitting. The width of the batches was set to 20, whereas the learning rate λ to 10^{-1}. The vector dimension D in the word embedding was 300, the regularization factor ℓ 10^{-4}, and the width of the hidden layer h 3000.

7 Results

The performance of the classifier presented in § 6 (named Enriched) was compared with a series of baselines. A naive baseline consists in always guessing the positive class (Positive). A more solid baseline is the state of the art for class-specific identification of implicit relations in the PDTB: the Shallow Convolutional Neural Network (SCNN) by Zhang et al. (2015). The configuration of this algorithm, as mentioned in § 3, includes max pooling, random under-sampling, and normalization. Finally, the last baseline is our

---

[3]Without random under-sampling, the algorithm worsened its performance, whereas no significant differences were observed with random over-sampling.

Classifier	Macro-F1	Precision	Recall	Accuracy
Positive	42.11	26.67	100	26.67
SCNN	52.04	39.80	75.29	63.00
Basic	53.01	42.04	71.74	**66.44**
Enriched	**54.52**	**42.37**	**76.45**	66.35

Classifier	Macro-F1	Precision	Recall	Accuracy
Positive	21.11	11.80	100	11.80
Basic	48.36	35.51	76.48	82.82
Enriched	**55.62**	**40.66**	**88.24**	**85.00**

Table 2: Different settings for the datasets PDTB (above) and CSTNews (below).

classifier deprived of the additional features (Basic): in other words, it hinges only upon the lexical features.

The results for both the PDTB and CSTNews datasets are presented in Table 2.[4] A McNamar's Chi-Squared test determined the statistical significance of the difference between the classes predicted by Enriched and Basic with $p < 0.05$. The enriched features have a positive impact on precision and recall. This effect is not always observed in accuracy: however, this metric is unreliable due to the high number of negative examples. The improvement on the PDTB is clearly related to implicit examples. From the results on the CSTNews corpus, however, it is safe to gather only that identification of causal relations in general is affected.

8 Conclusion

Drawing upon the semantic theory of events and inspired by work on related tasks, we enriched the feature set previously used for the identification of causal relations. Eventually, this set included lexical, positional, and event-related features. Providing this information to a Feedforward Neural Network, we obtained a series of results. Firstly, our method outperformed earlier approaches and solid baselines on two different datasets and in two different languages, demonstrating the benefit of enriched features. Secondly, our experiment confirmed two theoretical assumptions, namely the iconic principle and the complexity of events. In general, exploiting the theory of event semantics contributed significantly to discourse relation classification, demonstrating that these domains are intertwined to a certain extent.

---

[4]The results for the CSTNews corpus equals to the average of multiple initializations.

References

Priscila Aleixo and Thiago Alexandre Salgueiro Pardo. 2008. *CSTNews: um córpus de textos jornalísticos anotados segundo a teoria discursiva multidocumento CST (cross-document structure theory*. ICMC-USP.

Brandon Beamer and Roxana Girju. 2009. Using a bigram event model to predict causal potential. In *Computational Linguistics and Intelligent Text Processing*, pages 430–441. Springer.

Steven Bethard, William J. Corvey, Sara Klingenstein, and James H. Martin. 2008. Building a corpus of temporal-causal structure. In *Proceedings of LREC'16*, pages 908–915.

Bernd Bohnet. 2010. Very high accuracy and fast dependency parsing is not a contradiction. In *Proceedings of the 23rd international conference on computational linguistics*, pages 89–97.

Lynn Carlson, Mary Ellen Okurowski, Daniel Marcu, Linguistic Data Consortium, et al. 2002. *RST discourse treebank*. Linguistic Data Consortium, University of Pennsylvania.

Sonia Cristofaro. 2005. *Subordination*. Oxford University Press.

William Croft. 2002. *Typology and universals*. Cambridge University Press.

Holger Diessel and Katja Hetterle. 2011. Causal clauses: A cross-linguistic investigation of their structure, meaning, and use. *Linguistic universals and language variation*, pages 21–52.

Quang Xuan Do, Yee Seng Chan, and Dan Roth. 2011. Minimally supervised event causality identification. In *Proceedings of the Conference on Empirical Methods in Natural Language Processing*, pages 294–303.

David Dowty. 1991. Thematic proto-roles and argument selection. *Language*, 67(3):547–619.

Jesse Dunietz, Lori Levin, and Jaime Carbonell. 2015. Annotating causal language using corpus lexicography of constructions. In *The 9th Linguistic Annotation Workshop held in conjuncion with NAACL 2015*, pages 188–196.

Charles Fillmore. 1968. The case for case. In Emmon Bach and Robert Harms, editors, *Universals in linguistic theory*, pages 1–88. Holt, Rinehart & Winston.

Xavier Glorot and Yoshua Bengio. 2010. Understanding the difficulty of training deep feedforward neural networks. In *AISTATS*, volume 9, pages 249–256.

Cécile Grivaz. 2012. *Automatic extraction of causal knowledge from natural language texts*. Ph.D. thesis, University of Geneva.

John Haiman. 1985. Natural syntax. iconicity and erosion. *Cambridge Studies in Linguistics*, (44):1–285.

Sotaro Kita, N.J. Enfield, Jürgen Bohnemeyer, and James Essegbey. 2010. The macro-event property: The segmentation of causal chains. In J. Bohnemeyer and E. Pederson, editors, *Event representation in language and cognition*, pages 43–67. Cambridge University Press.

George Lakoff. 1984. Performative subordinate clauses. In *Annual Meeting of the Berkeley Linguistics Society*, volume 10, pages 472–480.

Ziheng Lin, Hwee Tou Ng, and Min-Yen Kan. 2014. A PDTB-styled end-to-end discourse parser. *Natural Language Engineering*, 20(02):151–184.

Paramita Mirza, Rachele Sprugnoli, Sara Tonelli, and Manuela Speranza. 2014. Annotating causality in the TempEval-3 corpus. In *Proceedings of the EACL 2014 Workshop on Computational Approaches to Causality in Language (CAtoCL)*, pages 10–19.

Joakim Nivre, Marie-Catherine de Marneffe, Filip Ginter, Yoav Goldberg, Jan Hajic, Christopher D Manning, Ryan McDonald, Slav Petrov, Sampo Pyysalo, Natalia Silveira, et al. 2016. Universal dependencies v1: A multilingual treebank collection. In *Proceedings of the 10th International Conference on Language Resources and Evaluation (LREC 2016)*, pages 1659–1666.

Ekaterina Ovchinnikova, Laure Vieu, Alessandro Oltramari, Stefano Borgo, and Theodore Alexandrov. 2010. Data-driven and ontological analysis of framenet for natural language reasoning. In *Proceedings of LREC'10*, pages 3157–3162.

Emily Pitler, Annie Louis, and Ani Nenkova. 2009. Automatic sense prediction for implicit discourse relations in text. In *Proceedings of the Joint Conference of the 47th Annual Meeting of the ACL and the 4th International Joint Conference on Natural Language Processing of the AFNLP: Volume 2*, pages 683–691.

Rashmi Prasad, Eleni Miltsakaki, Nikhil Dinesh, Alan Lee, Aravind Joshi, Livio Robaldo, and Bonnie L Webber. 2007. The Penn Discourse Treebank 2.0 annotation manual. Technical report.

James Pustejovsky, José M. Castano, Robert Ingria, Robert J. Gaizauskas, Andrea Setzer, Graham Katz, and Dragomir R. Radev. 2003. TimeML: Robust specification of event and temporal expressions in text. Technical report, AAAI.

Radim Řehůřek and Petr Sojka. 2010. Software Framework for Topic Modelling with Large Corpora. In *Proceedings of the LREC 2010 Workshop on New Challenges for NLP Frameworks*, pages 45–50, Valletta, Malta, May. ELRA. http://is.muni.cz/publication/884893/en.

Mehwish Riaz and Roxana Girju. 2013. Toward a better understanding of causality between verbal events: Extraction and analysis of the causal power of verb-verb associations. In *Proceedings of the annual SIGdial Meeting on Discourse and Dialogue (SIGDIAL)*, pages 21–30.

Caroline Sporleder and Alex Lascarides. 2008. Using automatically labelled examples to classify rhetorical relations: An assessment. *Natural Language Engineering*, 14(03):369–416.

Zeno Vendler. 1967. *Linguistics in philosophy*. Cornell University Press.

WenTing Wang, Jian Su, and Chew Lim Tan. 2010. Kernel based discourse relation recognition with temporal ordering information. In *Proceedings of the 48th Annual Meeting of the Association for Computational Linguistics*, pages 710–719.

Phillip Wolff. 2007. Representing causation. *Journal of experimental psychology: General*, 136(1):82.

Daojian Zeng, Kang Liu, Siwei Lai, Guangyou Zhou, Jun Zhao, et al. 2014. Relation classification via convolutional deep neural network. In *Proccedings of COLING'14*, pages 2335–2344.

Dongxu Zhang and Dong Wang. 2015. Relation classification via recurrent neural network. *arXiv preprint arXiv:1508.01006*.

Biao Zhang, Jinsong Su, Deyi Xiong, Yaojie Lu, Hong Duan, and Junfeng Yao. 2015. Shallow convolutional neural network for implicit discourse relation recognition. In *Proceedings of the 2015 Conference on Empirical Methods in Natural Language Processing*, pages 2230–2235.

Zhi-Min Zhou, Yu Xu, Zheng-Yu Niu, Man Lan, Jian Su, and Chew Lim Tan. 2010. Predicting discourse connectives for implicit discourse relation recognition. In *Proceedings of the 23rd International Conference on Computational Linguistics: Posters*, pages 1507–1514.

Stance Detection in Facebook Posts of a German Right-wing Party

Manfred Klenner and Don Tuggener and Simon Clematide
Computational Linguistics
University of Zurich, Switzerland
`{klenner,tuggener,siclemat}@cl.uzh.ch`

Abstract

We argue that in order to detect stance, not only the explicit attitudes of the stance holder towards the targets are crucial. It is the whole narrative the writer drafts that counts, including the way he hypostasizes the discourse referents: as benefactors or villains, as victims or beneficiaries. We exemplify the ability of our system to identify targets and detect the writer's stance towards them on the basis of about 100 000 Facebook posts of a German right-wing party. A reader and writer model on top of our verb-based attitude extraction directly reveal stance conflicts.

1 Introduction

Recently, verb-based sentiment relation extraction has been used among others to derive positive and negative attitudes of Democrats and Republicans towards actors or topics. The system of Rashkin et al. (2016) accomplishes this task on the basis of crowd-sourced connotation frames of (transitive) verbs which indicate such relations. A connotation frame specifies, among others, the polar effects a verb role bears, if the verb is used affirmatively.

We are also interested in stance detection, but *stance*, in our model, is not only the attempt to identify the positive and negative attitudes of the writer of the text (the main opinion holder) towards *given* actors (e.g. political parties) or (controversial) topics (henceforth targets) (see e.g. Mohammad et al. (2016)). We also strive to *identify* targets in the first place. We claim that the way the writer conceptualizes actors, namely as polarized actors - benefactors, villains, victims, beneficiaries (and so on) - reveals who/what the targets are. This also unveils, as a by-product, the writer's stance. A writer might not directly call someone a villain, but if he puts forward that a person has told a lie, then he obviously regards him as a villain, which implies a negative attitude.

We propose the following model. The writer produces - under the assumption of truth commitment - some text. The reader, on the basis of shared (lexical) semantic knowledge, is able to identify what the text implies for the various targets involved and described. The reader's personal preferences (his stance, his moral values etc.) might be affected by a given exposition. He might agree with the (implications of the) proclaimed facts or not. From what is being said, the reader is thus able to derive at least two things: How does the writer conceptualize the world (i.e. what is his stance, what are the targets) and how does this relate to the reader's stance. We focus on the interplay of these perspectives. Our model confronts the writer with the reader perspective. This way, conflicting conceptualizations of reality and incompatible stances become visible. This allows the reader to identify *charged* statements, i.e. main sources of disagreement.

We have implemented a system that predicts *advocate* and *adversary* attitudes and that further assigns sources and targets their polarized roles (benefactor, victim etc.) on the basis of a connotation verb lexicon comprising 1500 manually specified connotation frames stemming from 1100 different verbs, also including about hundred nominalisations. In order to do so, event factuality in the sense of Saurí and Pustejovsky (2009) also needs to be coped with.

In this paper, we are interested in a qualitative validation of our approach. On the basis of 100 000 Facebook posts of a right-wing German party, the AfD (Alternative für Deutschland), and a virtual (kind of prototypical) reader, we exemplify how conflicting perspectives can be identified and how stance is detected.

Proceedings of the 2nd Workshop on Linking Models of Lexical, Sentential and Discourse-level Semantics, pages 31–40,
Valencia, Spain, April 3, 2017. ©2017 Association for Computational Linguistics

2 Stance Detection: Ways to Go

Presumably, one finds directly expressed attitudes like *I hate Burger King* only in product reviews. In a political discourse, such aversions etc. are expressed more subtly. We are unlikely to find a sentence like *We, the AfD, are against refugees* in Facebook posts of AfD members. Then how can we get to know that this is apparently the case?[1] There are three ways how to identify the writer's stance.

1. Inference patterns (cf. exemplification E1). There are sentences, where *AfD* and *refugees* co-occur, but where the relation between them is given only indirectly.

E1: | If A0 is against an event that is good for A1, A0 is an adversary of A1 |

For example: *The AfD criticizes that refugees are tolerated by the German government.* Our model is able to derive an adversary relation between *AfD* and *refugee* from such complex sentences. The underlying inference pattern is: A negative attitude (*criticize*) of an opinion source (*AfD*) towards a situation (*tolerate*) that is positive for a target (*refugee*) means that an adversary relation holds between the two (*AfD* and *refugee*).

2. Inference chains (cf. E2).

Assume that our system derived that *refugee* is an adversary of *Germany*, and *AfD* is an advocate of *Germany* in the text. It then follows that *refugee* is an adversary of *AfD* and vice versa.

E2: | From: $A0_1$ is an adversary of A1
and: $A0_2$ is an advocate of A1
it follows that: $A0_1$ and $A0_2$ are adversaries |

We also tried to find cliques of accomplices of the main opinion source, here the AfD. Shared advocate or adversary relations help. For instance, from *AfD is an adversary of refugees* and *Pegida*[2] *is an adversary of refugees* it follows that the AfD is an advocate of Pegida.

3. Assignment of polar roles (cf. E3).

E3: | If a text has framed A0 as a villain then the writer is an adversary of A0 |

The majority of sentences in our corpus that contain *refugee* do not even mention the AfD explicitly. Nevertheless, some of them allow for the

---

inference of an adversary relation. All those sentences that imply that refugees are villains give rise to such an inference. If the writer conceptualizes someone as a villain, then he is an adversary of him. Clearly, this is defeasible, e.g. *He lied to me, but I still admire him.* This, however, must be done explicitly, otherwise we are entitled to assume an adversary relation. It is a distinctive component of our approach that we are able to determine such polar assignments. Their instantiation, however, must be licensed by the factuality or counterfactuality of events (cf. section 4).

Similarly, if someone conceptualizes someone as a victim, then he is - to a certain degree and maybe only situation-specific - an advocate of him, since normally victims do have our sympathy. Interestingly, the corresponding argumentation while true for benefactor, is not true for beneficiary. Someone who benefits from something could nevertheless be an adversary of us (we could take it as unjust that he benefits).

3 Attitudes and Polar Effects

According to Deng and Wiebe (2015) a verb might have a positive and a negative effect on the filler of the direct object, which they map to the patient or theme role. It is, however, not only the direct object that bears a polar connotation, but also the subject (e.g. *to whitewash*), the indirect object (di-transitive *to recommend*), the PP object (*to fight for*), and the complement clause (*to criticize that*). For German, we (Klenner and Amsler, 2016) have introduced a freely available verb lexicon which we called *sentiframes* (about 300 verb frames). For each verb, it specifies the positive and negative effects that the affirmative and factual use of the verb has on the filler objects on the basis of its grammatical functions. In case that a verb subcategorizes for a complement clause, the verb's implicature signature in the sense of Nairn et al. (2006) is specified as well. We have revised this resource[3] and substantially augmented it by adding 800 additional verbs, their frames (1200) and their verb signatures. We have also started to model verb derived nominalisations (e.g. *destruction*).

A sentiframe or connotation frame (we use the later term, henceforth) of a verb in our new model provides a mapping from argument positions (A0 etc.) to polar roles. We use two polar roles which

---

[1]We, the authors, use our knowledge as informed citizens in order to make such characterizations.

[2]Another xenophobic German movement.

[3]https://pub.cl.uzh.ch/projects/opinion/lrec_data.txt

we call *source* and *target*. Both roles are further qualified (verb specific) according to the polarity they bear. This is summarized in principle P1.

> P1: *source* and *target* are polar roles of verbs, they bear a positive or negative effect (or none)

Take for example the verb *whitewash*:

   A0 (source)   negative effect
   A1 (target)   positive effect

It is negatively connotated to whitewash (A0), while being whitewashed - at least given a naive point of view - is positive (A1).

A positive effect on the target indicates that the source either acts in a way that the target is positively affected (*cherish*), or it expresses a positive relationship directly (*admire*). Thus, principle P2 holds:

> P2: The type of attitude a verb expresses depends on the target role effect:
> *advocate* if positive, *adversary* if negative

The attitude relation is independent of the effect on the source (if any). We specify a function $\mathcal{R}$ (see Figure 1) that retrieves the attitude relation of a verb v given its affirmative status, i.e. $\textit{aff}(v) = 1$ if v is affirmative and 0 if negated. The function $\textit{teff}(v)$ retrieves the effect of verb v on its target role.

$$\mathcal{R}(v) =
\begin{cases}
\textit{adversary} & \text{if } \textit{teff}(v)=negative \wedge \textit{aff}(v) = 1 \\
\textit{adversary} & \text{if } \textit{teff}(v)=positive \wedge \textit{aff}(v) = 0 \\
\textit{advocate} & \text{if } \textit{teff}(v)=positive \wedge \textit{aff}(v) = 1 \\
\textit{advocate} & \text{if } \textit{teff}(v)=negative \wedge \textit{aff}(v) = 0
\end{cases}$$

Figure 1: Attitude Determination for Verbs

Depending on the affirmative and factuality status of the verb (event), the polar roles (see P1) turn into what we call a *polar assignment*.

> P3: *benefactor, villain, beneficiary, victim, pos_affected, neg_affected, ...* are polar assignments

For instance, given $A0_1$ *regrets that A1 has been insulted*, the negative target role of the verb *insult* gives rise to the polar assignment *victim*. The reason why we distinguish polar roles from polar assignments is that negation might alter the realization of a polar role.

> P4: The polar assignment (that a polar role gives rise to) depends on the affirmative status of the verb

For instance in *A1 was not rewarded*, the positive target role of A1 (target of *reward*) is, given verb negation, either neutralized or could even be interpreted as negative (A1 receives a negative effect). Note that an advocate relation between A0 and A1 does not necessarily imply that any of them receive a polar assignment. Given $A0_1$ *fears that $A0_2$ has insulted A1*, we have an advocate relation between $A0_1$ and A1. But neither is $A0_2$ a villain nor A1 a victim. In the context of *fears*, the truth value (factuality status) of the event denoted by *insult* is unknown.

> P5: Polar assignments occur if factuality or counterfactuality is given, but are blocked given non-factuality

In the case of a factual, but non-affirmative use of the verb, the situation is a bit more complicated, since negation might pragmatically be used in various ways, e.g. as a reproach (*We complain that A0 has not helped A1*) or as a plain denial (*We confirm that A0 has not criticized A1*). Only in a reproach the attitudes and the effects can safely be (partially) inverted. Given *A0 has not whitewashed A1* (meant as a denial), we might infer that this is negative for A1. But we certainly would not say that A0 has a negative attitude towards A1 nor that A0 should receive a positive effect (inverting the negative effect of the affirmative use).

The situation changes if we know that a statement is meant as a reproach, e.g. if it is embedded into a verb with a negative effect on its subclause, as in $A0_1$ *criticizes that $A0_2$ has not whitewashed A1*. We interpret this as a negative attitude of $A0_1$ towards $A0_2$ and a positive attitude of $A0_1$ towards A1. Here is the (partial) frame for *criticize* (A3 denotes a proposition):

   A0   no effect
   A3   negative effect

Note that in this example we have to combine two attitudes stemming from different verbs, namely *criticize* and *whitewash*.

> P6: An attitude towards an event might lead to a polar assignment for some roles of that event

An adversary relation on *whitewash* stemming from *criticize* combines with the adversary relation of *not whitewash* (=adversary) to give an advocate relation between $A0_1$ and $A1$. Figure 2 shows the definition of the function $\mathcal{C}$, which realizes relation composition. In the current example, the call would be: $\mathcal{C}(\mathcal{R}(criticize), \mathcal{R}(whitewash))$.

$$\mathcal{C}(r, s) = \begin{cases} adversary \text{ if } r = advocate \wedge s = adversary \\ advocate \text{ if } r = adversary \wedge s = adversary \\ adversary \text{ if } r = adversary \wedge s = advocate \\ advocate \text{ if } r = advocate \wedge s = advocate \end{cases}$$

Figure 2: Attitude Composition

P7:	Attitudes combine with attitudes to form a derived attitude

In P5, we saw that polar assignments depend on (counter-)factuality. We have not yet discussed how to determine (counter-)factuality. In the context of verbs that have clausal complements, we need a further notion, namely that of an implicature signature (Nairn et al., 2006). It relates to the truth or falsehood commitment that a verb casts on its clausal complement. The factuality of an event denoted by a clausal complement can be determined from the implicature commitment of the matrix verb, the affirmative status of the matrix verb and the affirmative status of the clausal complement. We discuss this in the next section. For the moment we postulate P8.

P8:	The polar assignment (that a polar role gives rise to) not only depends on the affirmative status of the verb, but also on the affirmative status and the implicature signature of the matrix verb

4 Truth Commitment, Negation, Factuality Status

We distinguish factual (true), counterfactual (not true) and non-factual (truth value is unknown). We call this the *factuality status* of an event denoted by a verb. In order to determine the factuality status of a clausal complement of a verb, its implicature signature and the affirmative status of the matrix and the subclause verb have to be taken into account. In order to specify the implicature signature, we use T, F, N for truth committed, falsehood committed, and no commitment, respectively, which is along the lines of Nairn et al. (2006), though not totally identical (e.g. they use *polarity* to denote what we call *affirmative status*).

For instance, *to regret* as a factive verb is truth committing (T), both in its affirmative and negated usage. Thus, the clausal complement of an instance of *to regret* is factual if affirmative, and counterfactual if negated. While *to refuse* is false-hood committing (F) if affirmatively used, there is no commitment (N) if negated. The clausal complement of negated *to refuse* thus is, in any case (i.e., affirmative or negated) non-factual.

In order to determine factuality, we first define a function $\mathcal{T}(v)$ which assigns a signature to a verb (especially with clausal complements) given the affirmative status of the verb. Figure 3 gives a (partial) definition of such a verb (class) specific mapping. Here, $aff(v) = 0$ (again) means that the verb v is negated, while $aff(v) = 1$ indicates an affirmative use of the verb.

$$\mathcal{T}(v) = \begin{cases} T & \text{if } v \in \{force, \ldots\} \wedge aff(v) = 1 \\ N & \text{if } v \in \{force, \ldots\} \wedge aff(v) = 0 \\ F & \text{if } v \in \{forget, \ldots\} \wedge aff(v) = 0 \\ T & \text{if } v \in \{forget, \ldots\} \wedge aff(v) = 1 \end{cases}$$

Figure 3: Implicature Signature

In order to determine the factuality of an event denoted by a subclause of a matrix verb, we apply the function defined in Figure 4. We use 'fact', 'cfact' and 'unk' for factual, counterfactual and unknown. Note that we interpret factuality as event factuality in the sense of Saurí and Pustejovsky (2009). The function m applied to the verb v delivers the embedding matrix verb.

$$\mathcal{S}(v) = \begin{cases} fact & \mathcal{T}(m(v)) = T \wedge aff(v) = 1 \\ cfact & \mathcal{T}(m(v)) = T \wedge aff(v) = 0 \\ fact & \mathcal{T}(m(v)) = F \wedge aff(v) = 1 \\ cfact & \mathcal{T}(m(v)) = F \wedge aff(v) = 0 \\ unk & \mathcal{T}(m(v)) = N \end{cases}$$

Figure 4: Factuality Determination

The main clause is non-factual if modals are present, otherwise it is factual or counterfactual. Negation turns the event denoted by the main verb into counterfactuality. Under counterfactuality as well as under factuality, polar assignments are licensed. Only if a main clause is non-factual, polar assignments are blocked.

Another distinctive feature of our approach is that not only clausal complements receive an implicature signature, but any verb role that could take a nominalisation as a filler receives one. Moreover, nominalisations themselves have signatures. We are not aware of any model that also considers these cases. Take: *He criticized the destruction of the monuments of Palmyra through Isis*. Here *destruction* is the direct object and there is a truth commitment stemming from *criticize*. The destruction, thus, is factual (affirmative use of *criticize*). Since *destruction* has 'T N' (= 'affirmative negated') as signature and since it is affirmative (T holds) Isis is recognized as a villain. If we take *to fear* instead of *to criticize*, this no longer holds. Also, if we add *supposed* or *postponed* to *destruction* (*supposed destruction*) we have 'N' as commitment and polar assignments are blocked.

The factuality status is determined outside-in. Slightly simplifying, we can say that in order to infer an attitude between actors, the verb (event) of A0 or the verb (event) of A1 must be factual or counterfactual. If both, A0 and A1 are arguments of the same verb, then it needs to be factual (A0 cheats A1). Counterfactuality (e.g. A0 no longer admires A1) might - depending on the verb or other indicators like *no longer* - also license an attitude derivation.

5 Reader Perspective

The *reader perspective* distinguishes opponents from proponents. These classes need to be specified in advance by the reader. For instance, he could select particular political parties or politicians as proponents. In our experiments described below, we created a virtual reader along the following lines. Our reader is a proponent of Europe, Merkel, Germany, refugees and so on and against the AfD. His values and aversions, hopes and fears are those of a typical member of the Western society, which we fixed in a reader profile that assigns polarities along the lines of the Appraisal theory (Martin and White, 2005), i.e. judgment, affect and appreciation. For instance, *honesty* is judgment positive and represents a moral value of the reader, while *terrorist* is a contemner of the reader's values. This lexicon[4] serves two purposes. It forms the basis of the reader's ability to understand what a text implies. But it also represents (or better approximates) his moral values, his aesthetic preferences, his emotional dispositions. He is able to discern that in *A0 approves terrorism* someone is an advocate of something he finds immoral or inhuman. Altogether, we have six roles for the reader perspective: *myValues, myAversions, mvValueConfirmer, myValueContemner, myProponent, myOpponent*.

Note that the instantiation of these roles (except myOpponent and myProponent) sometimes raise the need for sentiment composition (not only lexicon access). *terrorist* is a myValueContemner since the word - according to the lexicon - denotes a judgment negative animate entity. In order to classify *cheating colleague* as a myValueContemner of the reader, composition is needed. The judgment negative adjective *cheating* combined with the neutral noun *colleague*, which denotes an actor, gives rise to a judgment negative phrase denoting a myValueContemner of the reader. The phrase *sick minister*, on the other hand, although *minister* is an actor and *sick* is a negative word (but appreciation negative, not judgment), does not denote a myValueContemner, but a neutral entity.

6 Writer Perspective

The *writer perspective* tells the reader what the writer wants him to believe (to be true) and explicates what this implies for the status of the targets involved, i.e. whether they are benefactors etc. It is the way the writer conceptualizes the world through his text.

The roles stemming from the polar assignment, e.g. *victim, villain, benefactor and beneficiary* are actor roles related to the moral dimension (verb-specific), while the additional roles *pos_actor, neg_actor, pos_affected, neg_affected* are used for the remaining cases (roles of not morally loaded verbs).

Given a sentence, we combine the attitudes, the reader and the writer perspective into a single view. Formally, we instantiate the relation 5-tuple $\langle L_r, L_w, rel, L_r, L_w \rangle$ where L_R, L_w is the reader and writer perspective, respectively and rel represents the attitude of the source towards the target. The reader and writer view L_r and L_w are applied twice, to the source (left hand part of the 5-tuple) and the target (right hand part of the 5-tuple) connected by the (directed) attitude relation rel.

The writer perspective, L_w is determined by calling the function $\mathcal{A}(a, v)$ (see. Figure 5) with the verb v and the polar role a of the entity in question (target or source).

Given that *terrorist* is a value con-

---

[4]The lexicon is an adaptation of the lexicon described in Clematide and Klenner (2010).

$$\mathcal{A}(a,v) =$$

$$\begin{cases}
\textit{benefactor} & if & v \in \{\textit{help}..\} \wedge a = \textit{source} \\
& & \wedge\, \mathcal{S}(v) = \textit{fact} \\
\textit{beneficiary} & if & v \in \{\textit{help}..\} \wedge a = \textit{target} \\
& & \wedge\, \mathcal{S}(v) = \textit{fact} \\
\textit{villain} & if & v \in \{\textit{cheat}..\} \wedge a = \textit{source} \\
& & \wedge\, \mathcal{S}(v) = \textit{fact} \\
\textit{victim} & if & v \in \{\textit{cheat}..\} \wedge a = \textit{target} \\
& & \wedge\, \mathcal{S}(v) = \textit{fact} \\
\textit{victim} & if & v \in \{\textit{help}..\} \wedge a = \textit{target} \\
& & \wedge\, \mathcal{S}(v) = \textit{cfact} \\
\dots
\end{cases}$$

Figure 5: Polar Assignment

temner of the reader then *The politician helps the terrorist* would lead to the tuple $\langle$some,benefactor,advocate,myValueContemner,beneficiary$\rangle$ which reads: some benefactor is an advocate of a value contemner as a beneficiary. This immediately reveals the *charge* of the statement: a value contemner as a beneficiary. We could think of even more charged cases, e.g. a proponent of us as a villain. Or a proponent of us as an advocate of an opponent. Our tuple notation makes this transparent, it enables the search for such cases and we have defined secondary relations on top of it. We have identified 16 pattern that instantiate 4 new relations: new proponent, new opponent, no longer proponent and no longer opponent. A proponent of the reader who is an advocate of an opponent might no longer be a proponent etc. We give a couple examples in section 9.

7 Attitude Prediction

Given a sentence, we consider all pairs $\langle x, y \rangle$ such that x and y denote a noun position that acts as a polar role of one or more verbs. Given a pair of actors or entities, $\langle x, y \rangle$, both might occupy polar roles of the same or of different verbs. If x and y are arguments of the same verb, then, if factuality (or counterfactuality) holds, the attitude between them comes from the underlying verb. That is $\mathcal{R}(v)$ is applied if $\mathcal{S}(v) = $ 'fact' (or 'cfact').

If x and y have different verbal heads, i.e. the verbal head of x either directly or recursively embeds a verb with y as a polar role, then the relations stemming from the intermediary v_i are composed into a single relation rel (see Figure 2). If $A0_1$ *approves that* $A0_2$ *criticizes A1*, the relation between $A0_1$ and $A1$ is that of an adversary.

This depends on the advocate relation of *approve* and the adversary relation of *criticize*. Technically, we call $\mathcal{C}(\mathcal{R}(v), \mathcal{R}(v))$, depending on $\mathcal{S}(v)$. In general, we use a recursive function where attitude composition is performed outside-in along the lines just discussed. For instance, given $A0_1$ *criticizes that* $A0_2$ *does not help* $A1_1$ *to free* $A1_2$, we get: $\mathcal{C}(\mathcal{C}(\mathcal{R}(criticize), \mathcal{R}(help)), \mathcal{R}(free))$ which gives *adversary* (*criticize*) combined with *adversary* (negated *help*) which gives *advocate* which in turn is combined with *advocate* (*free*) which gives *advocate*: $A0_1$ advocate $A1_2$.

8 Sentiframes: Additional Details

The main components of a sentiframe or connotation frame are the effects that the source and target roles receive. We have shown that the actual assignments and relations also depend on the affirmative and factuality status. Of course, ambiguity is a problem. We found that shallow selectional restrictions distinguishing roles that require their filler to be an actor (persons, organizations, nations etc.) from roles where the filler must not be an actor actually help to reduce verb ambiguity. Other restrictions that are very useful are constraints that check the polarity of a filler object bottom-up. There are a couple of verbs that only (should) trigger if a bottom restriction is met. Take *prevent*: the one who prevents the solution of an urgent problem is a negative actor while if he prevents an assault, he is a hero. Other examples are verbs like *to call, to take*, e.g. *to call it a good/bad idea that* produces a positive or negative effect on the clausal complement. 95 connotation frames do have such bottom-up restrictions. We have implemented a straight-forward phrase-level sentiment composition (Moilanen and Pulman, 2007) in order to check bottom-up restrictions.

9 Example

Take the sentence (relevant positions are indexed): *The left-wing politician₃ criticized₄ that Merkel₆ helps₇ the refugees₉*. We get three pairs: $v_4{:}\langle x_3, y_6 \rangle, v_4{:}\langle x_3, y_9 \rangle$ and $v_7{:}\langle x_6, y_9 \rangle$. Let's say the reader has no prior attitudes towards left-wing politicians but that refugees has his sympathy (are *myProponents* of his). We discuss the case of $v_4{:}\langle x_3, y_9 \rangle$, i.e. the directed relation of the *left-wing politician* towards the *refugees*. The source of *criticize* has a negative attitude towards the *help* event. Since affirmative *help* represents an advo-

#	Relation Tuple	Illustration
1	⟨myProp,entity,adversary,myProp,neg_affected⟩	US refuses Germany something
2	⟨some,entity,is,adversary,of,myAversions,neg_affected⟩	someone condemns terror
3	⟨some,entity,is,advocate,of,myAversions,pos_affected⟩	someone insists on vengeance
4	⟨myProp,benefactor,advocate,myValContemner,beneficiary⟩	US supports dictator
5	⟨some,villain,adversary,myValues,neg_affected ⟩	someone ridicules human behavior

Table 1: Charged Relation Tuples

cate relation, we get adversary ∧ advocate = adversary (see Figure 2). The *left-wing politician* is just an entity, but the reader is a proponent of *refugees*. Since *help* is factual, *refugees* are beneficiaries. This yields:

⟨ some,entity,adversary,myProponent,beneficiary⟩.

We could paraphrase this as *some entity is an adversary of my proponent being a beneficiary*. Note that beneficiary as a role comes from factual *help*. This is the writer or text perspective. It tells us that the *refugees*, the reader proponents, are beneficiaries of some event that happened in reality. The relation also tells us that some entity is an adversary of this. That is, he does not approve the status of the reader's proponents, the refugees, as beneficiaries. This immediately makes him a candidate for the list of actors that are opponents of the reader.

Our tuple notation directly confronts the writer and the reader perspective and thus allows one to search for interesting cases. We have used a corpus comprising 3.5 million sentences taken from German periodicals (ZEIT and Spiegel) to explore this idea. Examples are given in table 1. The third column illustrates the underlying cases; US and Germany are set to be proponents of the reader (for short: *myProp*). In 1, two proponents are (surprisingly) adversaries. In 2, someone disapproves what the reader disapproves (a new proponent?). In 3, someone approves what the reader disapproves (a new opponent?). In 4, a proponent acts in a way the reader finds morally questionable (no longer a proponent?), and in 5, someone might turn out to be an opponent, since he violates the reader's values.

10 Empirical Evaluation

We have evaluated our approach quantitatively on the basis of 160 sentences. The data consists of 80 (rather complex) made-up sentences (one or more subclause embeddings) and 80 real sentences. Our goal was to verify the generative ca-

pacity of our model, thus the made-up sentences. It is much more convenient to invent complex sentences, where e.g. negation is permuted exhaustively over all subclauses, than to try to sample such rare constellations. Two annotators specified advocate and adversary relations and harmonized their annotations in order to get a gold standard.

Our goal was to see how our lexicon, including the principles of factuality determination, determines the performance. The precision was 83.5%, recall was 75.2%, which gives an F measure of 79.1%[5]. We then dropped the verb signatures from the lexicon, that is, we replaced the individual signatures by a default setting. There are three possible settings. We set the signature for the affirmative use of the verbs to 'T' (truth commitment), the signature for negated cases was set to 'F', 'N' and 'T' in turn. We got a precision of 69.06%, 75.36% and 74.88% and a recall of 69.36%, 71.62% and 75.2%. The F measure for the best default setting ('T T') is 75.06% which is about 4% points worse than the system's result, 79.1%. We also see that precision droped by 8% points which is a substantial loss. This demonstrates that verb-specific information is crucial.

Encouraged by these results, we decided to carry out a qualitative study in stance detection. We took 360 000 sentences from 100 000 Facebook posts of AfD members. Our system produced 44 000 polar facts from them: attitudes and polar assignments. Since these posts are (mostly) from AfD members, they implicitly represent their stance. The key messages, the self-conception of the party and the proclaimed friends and enemies should be accessible through these posts.

We aggregated polar facts by counting how often an actor was conceptualized as a villain etc., but also by counting the number of advocate and adversary relations between actors. We evaluated these aggregated polar facts through introspection.

---

[5]We use a dependency parser (Sennrich et al., 2009) and a rule-based predicate argument extractor, see Klenner and Amsler (2016) for the details

That is we relied on our knowledge about the AfD, its goals, methods, ideological stance etc. as portrayed by the mainstream German media.

The most important (since most frequent) polar fact derived by our systems already was in heart of the AfD's stance, namely that Angela Merkel, the German chancellor, is an adversary of Germany. That is exactly what the AfD claims. Actually, we get a very strong statement, in our tuple notation (recall that Merkel and Germany are reader proponents):

⟨myProponent,villain,adversary,myProponent,victim⟩

That is: myProponent (Merkel) as villain is an adversary of myProponent (Germany) as a victim. Conversely, these texts imply that the AfD is an advocate of Germany, that the refugees are adversaries of Germany, while the German government is an advocate of the refugees. Curiously enough, for the relation of the AfD towards refugees, we got inconsistent evidence (three times adversary, three times advocate). However, if we look at the polar assignment of refugees, which is villain, the picture is clear (see below). There are a couple of polar facts related to an event on New Year's Eve in 2015, where groups of men including migrants sexually assaulted women (that is the official statement). Our system came up with the polar fact that refugees are adversaries of (these) women.

Another question is, of course, who is to blame for the situation (in Germany). The mere fact that, in the perception of the AfD, Merkel is an adversary of Germany does not tell us whether this is positive or negative (in the eyes of the AfD). An adversary relation might be positive (e.g. A0 adversary terrorism), or negative (e.g. A0 adversary truth), i.e. the holder of the adversary attitude might be someone who shares or contemns our values, depending on the event underlying the adversary relation. If Merkel is said to cheat Germany, then the writer wants the reader to believe that Merkel is a villain and Germany her victim. Only then we know that the writer is (must be) an adversary of Merkel and an advocate of Germany.

In order to see who are villains and victims according to the AfD posts, we determined the most frequent actors that are classified as villains etc. To give a couple of examples: Among the villains are the refugees (ranked highest), immediately followed by Merkel and men (representing male refugees), the German word for villain itself (*Täter*) and government. We believe that these are

perfect hits. Victims are Germany, women (New Year's eve event), the AfD (presumably since misunderstood), and the citizen of Germany (AfD seems to believe: the government cheats the citizen). Among the beneficiaries are men (male refugees who are free to molest women without consequences), but also refugees (there is a welcome culture), Europe, criminals (since the government is weak) and the government. From these lists we can also see that the AfD conceptualizes itself as a victim, a positive actor and even a benefactor.

If someone is an adversary of the values of the reader, he might be a new opponent: we defined this and similar relations (no-longer-opponent) on top of our tuple notation. We found 80 different new opponent candidates, including various politicians, countries (their governments), parties, institutions (e.g. Nato) and concepts like *Flüchtlingswelle* (flood of refugees) or *politische Elite* (political elite). The list of entities we should no longer consider a proponent of the reader is perfect, it comprises Asylbewerber (refugee), Bundesregierung (government), Bundestag (parliament), EU, and Merkel. This exactly reflects the stance of the AfD.

11 Related Work

In this paper, stance detection is accomplished on the basis of opinion inference. A basic form of opinion inference is event evaluativity in the sense of Reschke and Anand (2011). They determine the polarity of an event as a function of the polarity of the arguments of the verb denoting the event. Work in the spirit of Reschke and Anand (2011) for the German language is described in Ruppenhofer and Brandes (2016a) and Ruppenhofer and Brandes (2016b). The goal of their approach is to create a verb-specific mapping from the prior attitude a so-called external viewer of an event has towards the verb arguments onto his overall evaluation of the event. For instance, if an immoral person lacks a good job, this is positive in the eye of the external viewer. Their approach focuses on a lexical resource, not on a system carrying out opinion inference. Thus, the authors do not take truth commitment, negation, and factuality determination into account. Nevertheless, their findings might be useful for what we call the reader perspective (where the prior polarity are needed).

A rule-based approach to sentiment implicatures (their term) is described in Deng and Wiebe (2015). This is the most recent and most elaborated version of a number of models of these authors. The goal is to detect entities that are in a positive or negative relation to each other. PosPair and NegPair are used as relation names, respectively. The model of Deng and Wiebe (2015) also copes with event-level sentiment inference, however factuality is not taken into account at all. Also, the reader is not modeled explicitly. Moreover, only attitude relations are derived, no polar assignments (beneficiary etc.) are modeled.

Recently, Rashkin et al. (2016) have presented an elaborate model that is meant to explicate the relations between all involved entities: the reader, the writer and the entities referred to by a sentence. Also, the internal states of the referents and their values are part of the model. The underlying resources, called connotation frames, were created in a crowd sourcing experiment, and the model parameter (e.g. values for positive and negative scores) are average values. Our resource, in contrast to such a layman's guess, was specified by an expert. The authors use belief propagation to induce the connotation frames of unseen verbs; they also use the connotation frames to predict entity polarities. This was applied to analyze the preferences and dispreferences of Democrats and Republicans. Choi et al. (2016) presented another application of that resource. Rashkin et al. (2016) claim to have a reader and a writer model, however, they do not seem to use it. This is in sharp contrast to our approach. Like Deng and Wiebe (2015), Rashkin et al. (2016) do not incorporate polar assignments (and factuality) in their model, which we deem crucial for stance detection.

Our previous model (Klenner, 2016; Klenner and Clematide, 2016) was realized with Description Logic OWL and the rule language SWRL (Horrocks and Patel-Schneider, 2004). The goal was to extract pro and contra relations from text. 42 SWRL rules were needed in order to establish such a functionality. In this paper, we have introduced a new model based on functions carrying out (a lean) attitude composition. We have also revised our approach for factuality determination. We now have a tripartite distinction while previously, our factuality labels were binary. The most important new feature of our current approach is the specification of our relation tuple which integrates the writer and the reader view.

A crucial difference of our model to existing approaches from the field of stance detection is that we do not only strive to classify the stance of a writer towards known controversial topics (e.g. abortion, climate change) like in e.g. Somasundaran and Wiebe (2010), Hasan and Ng (2014) or Anand et al. (2011). We also seek to identify the targets of the writer's stance in the first place. Among others, it is the way the writer frames the entities in his discourse (as villains etc.) that indicates his likes and dislikes.

12 Conclusions

We claim that the writer's conceptualization of reality as a narrative reveals his stance. In our case, the members of a political party together write that narrative which reflects how the AfD, a German right-wing party, divides the world into proponents and opponents, benefactors and villains and so. In contrast to previous approaches, we stress the point that an attitude between an opinion source and an opinion holder alone does not necessarily tell anything about how the writer perceives it. Only if we know the roles the source and the target play (e.g. villain, victim) in the whole discourse, we can identify the writer's stance towards them.

On a more technical level, the contributions of our approach are: 1200 new connotation frames for German, and a framework that integrates inferences both in verbal and nominal contexts. Our relation tuples jointly encode the reader and the writer perspective as well as the attitude among the source and target expressed by the underlying verb. Such a relation directly shows what the writer wants the reader to believe and how the reader - given his personal stances - might perceive this. This enables the reader to search for interesting constellations, where e.g. a proponent of his acts in an unexpected way.

Obvious future work stems from the need to define a more elaborated evaluation scenario. A small quantitative and an introspective qualitative evaluation was just a first (though successful) step.

Acknowledgments

We would like to thank Felix Michel and Simon Wörpel (https://correctiv.org), who sampled the corpus of Facebook posts.

References

Pranav Anand, Marilyn Walker, Rob Abbott, Jean E. Fox Tree, Robeson Bowmani, and Michael Minor. 2011. Cats rule and dogs drool!: Classifying stance in online debate. In *Proceedings of the 2nd Workshop on Computational Approaches to Subjectivity and Sentiment Analysis (WASSA)*, pages 1–9, Portland, Oregon, USA.

Eunsol Choi, Hannah Rashkin, Luke Zettlemoyer, and Yejin Choi. 2016. Document-level sentiment inference with social, faction, and discourse context. In *Proceedings of the 54th Annual Meeting of the Association for Computational Linguistics (ACL)*, pages 333–343, Berlin, Germany, August.

Simon Clematide and Manfred Klenner. 2010. Evaluation and extension of a polarity lexicon for German. In *Proceedings of the First Workshop on Computational Approaches to Subjectivity and Sentiment Analysis (WASSA)*, pages 7–13, Lisbon, Portugal.

Lingjia Deng and Janyce Wiebe. 2015. Joint prediction for entity/event-level sentiment analysis using probabilistic soft logic models. In *Proceedings of the 2015 Conference on Empirical Methods in Natural Language Processing (EMNLP)*, pages 179–189, Lisbon, Portugal.

Kazi Saidul Hasan and Vincent Ng. 2014. Why are you taking this stance? Identifying and classifying reasons in ideological debates. In *Proceedings of the 2014 Conference on Empirical Methods in Natural Language Processing (EMNLP)*, pages 751–762, Doha, Qatar.

Ian Horrocks and Peter F. Patel-Schneider. 2004. A proposal for an OWL rules language. In *Proceedings of the Thirteenth International World Wide Web Conference (WWW)*, pages 723–731, New York, NY, USA.

Manfred Klenner and Michael Amsler. 2016. Sentiframes: A resource for verb-centered German sentiment inference. In Nicoletta Calzolari (Conference Chair), Khalid Choukri, Thierry Declerck, Sara Goggi, Marko Grobelnik, Bente Maegaard, Joseph Mariani, Helene Mazo, Asuncion Moreno, Jan Odijk, and Stelios Piperidis, editors, *Proceedings of the Tenth International Conference on Language Resources and Evaluation (LREC)*, pages 2888–2891, Portoro, Slovenia.

Manfred Klenner and Simon Clematide. 2016. How factuality determines sentiment inferences. In Ivan Titov Claire Gardent, Raffaella Bernardi, editor, *Proceedings of *SEM 2016: The Fith Joint Conference on Lexical and Computational Semantics*, pages 75–84, Berlin, Germany, August.

Manfred Klenner. 2016. A model for multi-perspective opinion inferences. In Carlo Strapparava Larry Birnbaum, Octavian Popescu, editor, *Proceedings of IJCAI Workshop Natural Language Meets Journalism*, pages 6–11, New York, USA.

James R. Martin and Peter R. R. White. 2005. *Appraisal in English*. Palgrave Macmillan, London, England.

Saif Mohammad, Svetlana Kiritchenko, Parinaz Sobhani, Xiao-Dan Zhu, and Colin Cherry. 2016. SemEval task 6: Detecting stance in tweets. In *Proceedings of the 10th International Workshop on Semantic Evaluation (SemEval)*, pages 31–41, San Diego, CA, USA.

Karo Moilanen and Stephen Pulman. 2007. Sentiment composition. In *Recent Advances in Natural Language Processing (RANLP)*, pages 378–382, Borovets, Bulgaria.

Rowan Nairn, Cleo Condoravdi, and Lauri Karttunen. 2006. Computing relative polarity for textual inference. In *Proceedings of Inference in Computational Semantics (ICoS 5)*, pages 67–75, Buxton, England.

Hannah Rashkin, Sameer Singh, and Yejin Choi. 2016. Connotation frames: A data-driven investigation. In *Proceedings of the 54th Annual Meeting of the Association for Computational Linguistics (ACL)*, pages 311–321, Berlin, Germany, Angust.

Kevin Reschke and Pranav Anand. 2011. Extracting contextual evaluativity. In *Proceedings of the Ninth International Conference on Computational Semantics (IWCS)*, pages 370–374, Oxford, England.

Josef Ruppenhofer and Jasper Brandes. 2016a. Effect functors for opinion inference. In Nicoletta Calzolari (Conference Chair), Khalid Choukri, Thierry Declerck, Sara Goggi, Marko Grobelnik, Bente Maegaard, Joseph Mariani, Helene Mazo, Asuncion Moreno, Jan Odijk, and Stelios Piperidis, editors, *Proceedings of the Tenth International Conference on Language Resources and Evaluation (LREC)*, pages 2879–2887, Portoro, Slovenia, May.

Josef Ruppenhofer and Jasper Brandes. 2016b. Verifying the robustness of opinion inference. In Stefanie Dipper, Friedrich Neubarth, and Heike Zinsmeister, editors, *Proceedings of the 13th Conference on Natural Language Processing (KONVENS)*, pages 226–235. Bochum, Germany.

Roser Saurí and James Pustejovsky. 2009. FactBank: a corpus annotated with event factuality. *Language Resources and Evaluation*, 43(3):227–268.

Rico Sennrich, Gerold Schneider, Martin Volk, and Martin Warin. 2009. A new hybrid dependency parser for German. In *Proceedings of the German Society for Computational Linguistics and Language Technology (GSCL)*, pages 115–124, Potsdam, Germany.

Swapna Somasundaran and Janyce Wiebe. 2010. Recognizing stances in ideological on-line debates. In *Proceedings of the NAACL HLT 2010 Workshop on Computational Approaches to Analysis and Generation of Emotion in Text*, pages 116–124, Los Angeles, California, USA.

Behind the Scenes of an Evolving Event Cloze Test

Nathanael Chambers
Department of Computer Science
United States Naval Academy
`nchamber@usna.edu`

Abstract

This paper analyzes the narrative event cloze test and its recent evolution. The test removes one event from a document's chain of events, and systems predict the missing event. Originally proposed to evaluate learned knowledge of event scenarios (e.g., scripts and frames), most recent work now builds ngram-like language models (LM) to beat the test. This paper argues that the test has slowly/unknowingly been altered to accommodate LMs. Most notably, tests are auto-generated rather than by hand, and no effort is taken to include core script events. Recent work is not clear on evaluation goals and contains contradictory results. We implement several models, and show that the test's bias to high-frequency events explains the inconsistencies. We conclude with recommendations on how to return to the test's original intent, and offer brief suggestions on a path forward.

1 Introduction

A small but growing body of work is looking at learning real-world event knowledge. One particular area is how to induce event structures called schemas, scripts, or frames. This is a wide field, but variations on the narrative cloze test are often used to evaluate learned models. However, their current form has evolved beyond the cloze's original purpose. It has evolved into a language modeling (LM) task rather than an evaluation of knowledge. One proposal suggested avoiding the cloze test absent other options (Rudinger et al., 2015), but we argue that it can be useful if care-

fully formulated. This is the first paper to evaluate *why* LMs can seemingly succeed on the event cloze. This is also the first paper to reconcile contradictory results across recent papers. We reproduce several models for cloze prediction, include a new instance-based learning model, and show how high-frequency events pollute the test. We conclude by discussing the future of the cloze in regards to new corpus developments.

2 Previous Work

2.1 The Original Narrative Event Cloze

The narrative event cloze task was first proposed in Chambers and Jurafsky (2008). These papers introduced the first models that automatically induced event structures like Schankian scripts from unlabeled text. They learned chains of events that form common-sense structures. An event was defined as a verb/dependency tuple where the main entity in a story (the protagonist) filled the typed dependency of the verb. The following is an example with its corresponding event chain:

Text
The police arrested Jon but he escaped.
Jon fled the country.
Chain
(arrested, object), (escaped, subj), (fled, subj)

This is one instance of a chain. Research focuses on generalizing this knowledge to a stereotypical script of when a suspect escapes. In order to evaluate this generalized knowledge, the narrative cloze was proposed as one possible test. Given a set of known events, the test removes one, and a system must predict which was removed. Using the same short example:

(arrested, object), (escaped, subject), (____, ____)

Proceedings of the 2nd Workshop on Linking Models of Lexical, Sentential and Discourse-level Semantics, pages 41–45,
Valencia, Spain, April 3, 2017. ©2017 Association for Computational Linguistics

A model of scripts can produce a ranked list of likely events to fill the hole. The test evaluates where in the ranking the correct event is found. Critically, these event tests were *manually* extracted from *hand-selected* documents.

2.2 Language Modeling Event Cloze

Jans et al. (2012) focused solely on the narrative cloze test as an end goal. They cited the cloze evaluation from Chambers and Jurafsky (2008), but made several cloze modifications that we argue make it more amenable to language modeling. Since then, subsequent work has adopted the Jans evoluation of the cloze test. There are three main changes to the original **Narrative cloze** that turned it into an **LM cloze**.

Automatic Tests: First, the LM cloze tests are *automatically generated* with all the mistakes of parsers and coreference. The original narrative cloze was manually created by human annotators who interpreted documents and extracted sets of events by hand. Accuracy was "true accuracy", and it tested only one central chain in each document. It is not clear why everyone switched to LM cloze, but Jans et al. (2012) is revealing, *"Rather than manually constructing a set of scripts on which to run the cloze test, we ... use the event chains from that section as the scripts for which the system must predict events."* Their version is not the narrative cloze from Chambers and Jurafsky. This change created what is often desired: a quick automated test with instant results.

Text Order: The LM cloze is an evaluation where events are *ordered* to know the text position of the missing event. The original narrative cloze did not require ordering information because document order does not imply real-world order, and scripts focused on real-world structure. This change naturally benefits text language models.

All Chains: Instead of selecting the central entity in a document and testing that scenario's chain, they included all entity chains. Different papers vary on this detail, but all appear to auto-extract multiple chains per document. Some include minimum chain length requirements.

All Events: Fourth, the LM cloze includes all repeated events in a chain. If an event chain contains 5 'said' events, 5 cloze tests with the same answer 'said' are in the evaluation. Critically, variants of

'said' make up 20% of the data. The original cloze only included unique events without repetition. It also intentionally omitted all 'be' events, avoiding another frequent/uninformative event in the tests (Chambers and Jurafsky, 2008). To clearly illustrate the problem, below is one such LM cloze test:

X criticized, X said, X distributed, X asking, X said, X said, X said, X said, X admitted, X asked

The narrative cloze would only test one *X said* instead of five. This seemingly small evaluation detail drops a unigram model's 'said' prediction from 50% (5 of 10) to 17% (1 of 6) accuracy.

Subsequent work adopted these changes. Pichotta and Mooney (2014) proposed a multi-argument language model. They showed that bigrams which take into account all entity arguments can outperform bigrams that only use a single argument. Rudinger et al. (2015) showed that a log-bilinear language model outperforms bigram models on the same LM cloze. Several have proposed neural network LMs (Pichotta and Mooney, 2016; Modi, 2016). Granroth-Wilding and Clark (2016) made the cloze a multiple choice prediction rather than a ranking. Curiously, they auto-generated *one* chain per document instead of all chains, and required that chain to be at least 9 events in length. Ahrendt and Demberg (2016) build on the n-gram models with argument typing and use the cloze test on a non-news corpus.

Notably with these variations, results across papers contradict. A frequency baseline is the best in some, but not in others. A PMI-based counting approach is poor in some, but close to state-of-the-art in others. Rudinger et al.'s best LM leads them to conclude that either (1) script induction should use LMs, or (2) the cloze should be abandoned. We argue instead for a third option: the LM cloze should find its way back to the original intent.

3 Data Processing

To be consistent with recent work, we use the English Gigaword Corpus for training and test. We parse into typed dependencies with the CoreNLP toolkit, run coreference, and extract event chains connected by a single entity's mentions. Each coreference entity then extracts its event chain, made up of the predicates in which it is a subject, object, or preposition argument. An event is a tuple similar to Pichotta and Mooney (2014): (s, o, p, event) where s/o/p are the subject, object, and preposition unique entity IDs. Entity singletons are ignored, and *all* chains of length 2 or above are extracted as in these recent works.

4 Models

In order to ground our argument in the correct context, we implemented the main models from Chambers and Jurafsky (Chambers and Jurafsky, 2008), Jans et al. (2012), and Pichotta and Mooney (2014). Others have been proposed, but these core models are sufficient to illustrate the idiosyncrasies shared by LMs on event cloze prediction.

4.1 Unigrams

The unigram model is based on frequency counts from training. We define a similarity score for an event e in a chain of events c at insertion index k:

$$sim_u(e, c, k) = C(e)/N \qquad (1)$$

where $C(e)$ is the count of event e and N is the number of events seen in training.

4.2 Bigrams

The bigram model is formulated as an ordered text equation as in Jans et al. (2012):

$$sim_b(e, c, k) = \prod_{i=0}^{k} P(e|c_i) * \prod_{i=k+1}^{n} P(c_i|e) \qquad (2)$$

where the conditional probability is defined:

$$P(x|y) = \frac{C(x, y) + \lambda}{C(y) + |E| * \lambda} \qquad (3)$$

where $C(x, y)$ is the text ordered bigram count, E is the set of events, and λ a smoothing parameter.

4.3 PMI

Pointwise mutual information was the central component of Chambers and Jurafsky (2008). They learned a variety of script/event knowledge including argument type information that is not necessarily evaluated in the LM cloze. However, for consistency, previous work tends to duplicate their prediction model as follows:

$$sim_p(e, c, k) = \sum_{i=0}^{n} log \frac{P(c_i, e)}{P(c_i)P(e)} \qquad (4)$$

where the joint probability is defined:

$$P(x, y) = \frac{C(x, y) + C(y, x)}{\sum_i \sum_j C(e_i, e_j)} \qquad (5)$$

Jans et al. (2012) propose an *ordered* PMI that we omit for simplicity. They found that ordering doesn't affect PMI (but is required for bigrams).

4.4 Multi-Argument N-Gram Models

The above models use a single entity in a chain (arrested X, X escaped, X fled). Pichotta and Mooney (2014) explored richer models that consider all arguments with the events. The single chain now becomes (Y arrested X, X escaped, X fled Z). If other entities are repeated across events, it uses the same variable/ID so that coreference can be modeled beyond the main entity. The n-gram models are slightly more complicated now that arguments need to be normalized, particularly in how events are counted and how the conditional probability is computed. We refer the reader to their paper for a complete formulation.

This richer formulation has not been adopted by later work, possibly due to its complexity, but we duplicated their models for completeness.

4.5 Instance-Based N-Grams

We also propose a novel extension to previous work in an attempt to not just duplicate performance, but maximize its results. Instead of training on all documents, we train *on-the-fly* with an instance-based learning approach. Given a chain of events, the algorithm retrieves documents in Gigaword that contain all the events, and computes counts $C(x)$ and $C(x, y)$ only from that subset of documents. A parameter can be tuned to require X% of the chain events to match in a document. We duplicated both unigrams and bigrams (as above) with this on-the-fly training method.

5 Experiment Setup

There are two ways to evaluate event prediction with scripts. The first is to follow a single actor through a chain of events, and predict the missing link in the chain. This prediction ignores other event arguments and only evaluates whether the system predicts the predicate and the correct syntactic position of the entity. This was part of the original *narrative cloze* from Chambers and Jurafsky (2008). The example in Section 2 illustrates such a chain. Pichotta and Mooney (Pichotta and Mooney, 2014) proposed a richer test that requires all arguments of the missing event. A single actor is still tracked through a chain of events, but correct prediction requires the complete event.

We trained on 12.5 million AP documents from Gigaword with duplicates removed. The test set is 1000 random event chains not in training. Parameters were tuned on a smaller set of dev documents.

Single Argument Chains

Model	Recall@50
Unigrams	0.338
Uni Exact 100%	0.347
Uni Exact 50%	0.386
Bigrams (k=2)	0.465
Bi Exact 100% (k=2)	0.460
PMI	0.038
PMI w/cutoff	0.391

Table 1: Single entity event chain results.

Multiple Argument Chains

Model	Recall@50
Unigrams	0.322
Uni Exact 100%	0.332
Uni Exact 50%	0.368
Bigrams (k=5)	0.408
Bi Exact 100% (k=5)	0.396
PMI	0.068
PMI w/cutoff	0.364

Table 2: Multiple argument event chain results.

6 Results

Table 1 shows model performance. The best unigram model used our new instance-based learning, but bigrams gain by 8% absolute. Notably, **PMI** performs poorly as in Jans et al. (2012) and Rudinger et al. (2015). However, by adding a frequency cutoff, *the poor result is reversed*. Figure 1 shows the cutoff recall curve. Both papers concluded that PMI was the problem, but we found it is simply the *over*-evaluation of frequent events.

PMI is known to prefer infrequent events, and this is evident by looking at the *information content* (IC) of model predictions. The information content of an event is its log probability in the Gigaword Corpus. What types of events do language models predict? Table 3 shows that the average LM prediction contains far less information. Perhaps more clear, Table 4 shows an actual list of predictions for one cloze test. The n-gram models predict frequent events, but PMI predicts seemingly more meaningful events. We are not arguing in favor of PMI as a model, but simply illustrating how frequency explains almost all of the contradictions in previous work.

Finally, Table 2 mirrors the relative results of single arguments in the multi-argument setting. Once again, a simple cutoff parameter in the PMI

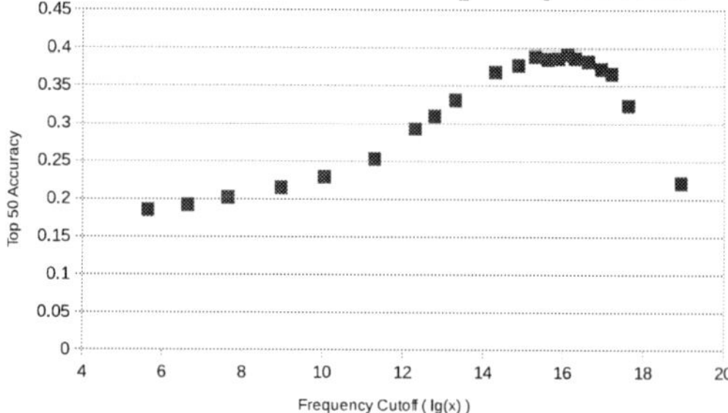

Figure 1: Frequency cutoffs. Events seen less than the cutoff are not included in the PMI ranking.

Unigrams	Bigrams	PMI
5.8	6.7	**9.4**

Table 3: Avg. information content of predictions.

setting drastically changes the results. It is difficult to always know what settings were used in each attempt at this task, but the normalized experiments in this paper illustrate that the new cloze experiments have a heavy bias to the high-frequency events, regardless of how the events themselves are formalized (e.g., single argument or multi argument).

7 Conclusion and Recommendations

Automatically generating event chains for evaluation does not test *relevant* script knowledge. The information content scores illustrate the huge extent to which common events (said, tell, went) dominate. More concerning, we can simply adjust the frequency cutoff in PMI learning, and it eliminates "poor results" from multiple previous papers. Language modeling approaches tend to capture frequent event patterns, not script knowledge.

Cloze Test	Unigram	Bigram	PMI
X scored	X said	X made	X scored
X set up	X have	X said	X beat
X headed	X had	X scored	X played
X challenged	told X	X accused	X missed
_____??_____	X told	X had	X hit
	X is	told X	X led
	X was	X told	X joined
	said X	X is	X went
	X has	X was	X finished
	killed X	said X	X opened

Table 4: Example Cloze test and the top predictions from ngrams and PMI

This is revealed in our frequency-based results, as well as in subjective error analysis like Table 4.

The core problem is that auto-generation does not evaluate script knowledge. We can't include all coreference chains from all documents and hope that this somehow measures script knowledge. The contradictory results from frequent events is just a symptom of the larger problem. We believe a *human annotator* should be in the loop for a meaningful evaluation. The test should include *meaningful core events*, and avoid others that are not script-relevant, such as discourse-related events (e.g., reporting verbs). Further, the test must not include events brought in through parser and coreference errors. By evaluating on parser output as gold data, we evaluate how well our models match our flawed text pre-processing tools. We acknowledge that human involvement is expensive, but the current trend to automate evaluations does not appear to be evaluating common-sense knowledge.

Finally, although this paper focuses on the narrative event cloze, we recognize that different evaluations are also possible. However, the traits of *human-annotation* and *core-events* seem to be required. One interesting task this year is Mostafazadeh et al. (2016) and the *Story Cloze* (manually created). Different from event chains, it still meets the requirements and provides a very large common corpus with 100k short stories. Another recent proposal is the InScript Corpus from Modi et al. (2016). They used Amazon Turk to create 1000 stories covering 10 predefined scenarios. While not as large and diverse as the Story Cloze, the entire corpus was annotated for gold events, coreference, and entities. This is an interesting new resource that avoids many of the problems discussed above, although issues of an event's *coreness* to a narrative may still need to be addressed.

We ultimately hope this short paper helps clarify recent results, inspires future evaluation, and most of all encourages discussion.

Acknowledgments

This work was supported by a grant from the Office of Naval Research.

References

Simon Ahrendt and Vera Demberg. 2016. Improving event prediction by representing script participants. In *Proceedings of North American Chapter of the Association for Computational Linguistics*.

Nathanael Chambers and Dan Jurafsky. 2008. Unsupervised learning of narrative event chains. In *Proceedings of the Association for Computational Linguistics (ACL)*, Hawaii, USA.

Mark Granroth-Wilding and Stephen Clark. 2016. What happens next? event prediction using a compositional neural network model. In *Proceedings of the 13th AAAI Conference on Artificial Intelligence*.

Bram Jans, Steven Bethard, Ivan Vulić, and Marie Francine Moens. 2012. Skip n-grams and ranking functions for predicting script events. In *Proceedings of the 13th Conference of the European Chapter of the Association for Computational Linguistics*, pages 336–344. Association for Computational Linguistics.

Ashutosh Modi, Tatjana Anikina, Simon Ostermann, and Manfred Pinkal. 2016. Inscript: Narrative texts annotated with script information. In *Proceedings of the 10th International Conference on Language Resources and Evaluation (LREC 16), Portoroz, Slovenia*, pages 3485–3493.

Ashutosh Modi. 2016. Event embeddings for semantic script modeling. In *Proceedings of the the SIGNLL Conference on Computational Natural Language Learning (CoNLL)*.

Nasrin Mostafazadeh, Nathanael Chambers, Xiaodong He, Devi Parikh, Dhruv Batra, Lucy Vanderwende, Pushmeet Kohli, and James Allen. 2016. A corpus and cloze evaluation for deeper understanding of commonsense stories. In *Proceedings of North American Chapter of the Association for Computational Linguistics*.

Karl Pichotta and Raymond J. Mooney. 2014. Statistical script learning with multi-argument events. In *Proceedings of the 14th Conference of the European Chapter of the Association for Computational Linguistics (EACL 2014)*, Gothenburg, Sweden, April.

Karl Pichotta and Raymond J. Mooney. 2016. Learning statistical scripts with LSTM recurrent neural networks. In *Proceedings of the 30th AAAI Conference on Artificial Intelligence (AAAI-16)*, Phoenix, Arizona.

Rachel Rudinger, Pushpendre Rastogi, Francis Ferraro, and Benjamin Van Durme. 2015. Script induction as language modeling. In *Proceedings of the 2015 Conference on Empirical Methods in Natural Language Processing (EMNLP-15)*.

LSDSem 2017 Shared Task: The Story Cloze Test

Nasrin Mostafazadeh[1], Michael Roth[2,3], Annie Louis[4],
Nathanael Chambers[5], James F. Allen[1,6]

1 University of Rochester   2 University of Illinois at Urbana-Champaign   3 University of Edinburgh

4 University of Essex   5 United States Naval Academy   6 Florida Institute for Human & Machine Cognition

`{nasrinm,james}@cs.rochester.edu`   `mroth@coli.uni-saarland.de`

`aplouis@essex.ac.uk`   `nchamber@usna.edu`

Abstract

The LSDSem'17 shared task is the Story Cloze Test, a new evaluation for story understanding and script learning. This test provides a system with a four-sentence story and two possible endings, and the system must choose the correct ending to the story. Successful narrative understanding (getting closer to human performance of 100%) requires systems to link various levels of semantics to commonsense knowledge. A total of eight systems participated in the shared task, with a variety of approaches including end-to-end neural networks, feature-based regression models, and rule-based methods. The highest performing system achieves an accuracy of 75.2%, a substantial improvement over the previous state-of-the-art.

1 Introduction

Building systems that can understand stories or can compose meaningful stories has been a long-standing ambition in natural language understanding (Charniak, 1972; Winograd, 1972; Turner, 1994; Schubert and Hwang, 2000). Perhaps the biggest challenge of story understanding is having commonsense knowledge for comprehending the underlying narrative structure. However, rich semantic modeling of the text's content involving words, sentences, and even discourse is crucially important. The workshop on Linking Lexical, Sentential and Discourse-level Semantics (LSD-Sem)[1] is committed to encouraging computational models and techniques which involve multiple levels of semantics.

---

[1] `http://www.coli.uni-saarland.de/` `~mroth/LSDSem/`

The LSDSem'17 shared task is the Story Cloze Test (SCT; Mostafazadeh et al., 2016). The SCT is one of the recent proposed frameworks on evaluating story comprehension and script learning. In this test, the system reads a four-sentence story along with two alternative endings. It is then tasked with choosing the correct ending. Mostafazadeh et al. (2016) summarize the outcome of experiments conducted using several models including the state-of-the-art script learning approaches. They suggest that current methods are only slightly better than random performance and more powerful models will require richer modeling of the semantic space of stories.

Given the wide gap between human (100%) and state-of-the-art system (58.5%) performance, the time was ripe to hold the first shared task on SCT. In this paper, we present a summary on the first organized shared task on SCT with eight participating systems. The submitted approaches to this non-blind challenge ranged from simple rule-based methods, to linear classifiers and end-to-end neural models, to hybrid models that leverage a variety of features on different levels of linguistic analysis. The highest performing system achieves an accuracy of 75.2%, which substantially improves the previously established state-of-the-art. We hope that our findings and discussions can help reshape upcoming evaluations and shared tasks involving story understanding.

2 The Story Close Test (SCT)

In the SCT task, the system should choose the right ending to a given four-sentence story. Hence, this task can be seen as a reading comprehension test in which the binary choice question is always, 'Which of the two endings is the most plausible correct ending to the story?'. Table 1 shows three example SCT cases.

Proceedings of the 2nd Workshop on Linking Models of Lexical, Sentential and Discourse-level Semantics, pages 46–51,
Valencia, Spain, April 3, 2017. ©2017 Association for Computational Linguistics

Context	Right Ending	Wrong Ending
Sammy's coffee grinder was broken. He needed something to crush up his coffee beans. He put his coffee beans in a plastic bag. He tried crushing them with a hammer.	It worked for Sammy.	Sammy was not that much into coffee.
Gina misplaced her phone at her grandparents. It wasnt anywhere in the living room. She realized she was in the car before. She grabbed her dads keys and ran outside.	She found her phone in the car.	She didnt want her phone anymore.
Sarah had been dreaming of visiting Europe for years. She had finally saved enough for the trip. She landed in Spain and traveled east across the continent. She didn't like how different everything was.	Sarah decided that she preferred her home over Europe.	Sarah then decided to move to Europe.

Table 1: Example Story Cloze Test instances from the Spring 2016 release.

Story Title	Story
The Hurricane	Morgan and her family lived in Florida. They heard a hurricane was coming. They decided to evacuate to a relative's house. They arrived and learned from the news that it was a terrible storm. They felt lucky they had evacuated when they did.
Marco Votes For President	Marco was excited to be a registered voter. He thought long and hard about who to vote for. Finally he had decided on his favorite candidate. He placed his vote for that candidate. Marco was proud that he had finally voted.
Spaghetti Sauce	Tina made spaghetti for her boyfriend. It took a lot of work, but she was very proud. Her boyfriend ate the whole plate and said it was good. Tina tried it herself, and realized it was disgusting. She was touched that he pretended it was good to spare her feelings.

Table 2: Example ROCStories instances from the Winter 2017 release.

As described in Mostafazadeh et al. (2016), the SCT cases are collected through Amazon Mechanical Turk (Mturk) on the basis of the ROCStories corpus, a collection of five-sentence everyday life stories which are full of stereotypical sequence of events. To construct SCT cases, they randomly sampled complete five-sentence stories from the ROCStories corpus and presented only the first four sentences of each story to the Mturk workers. Then, for each story, a worker was asked to write a 'right ending' and a 'wrong ending'. This resulting set was further filtered by human verification: they compile each SCT case into two independent five-sentence stories, once with the 'right ending' and once with the 'wrong ending'. Then, for each story they asked three crowd workers to verify if the given five-sentence story makes sense as a meaningful story, rating on the scale of {-1, 0, 1}. Then they retain the cases in which the 'right ending' had three 1 ratings and the 'wrong ending' had three 0 ratings. This verification step ensures that there are no boundary cases of 'right ending' and 'wrong ending' for human. Finally, any stories used in creating this SCT set are removed from the original ROCStories corpus.

3 Shared Task Setup

For the shared task, we provided the same dataset as created by Mostafazadeh et al. (2016), which consists of a development and test set each containing 1,871 stories with two alternative endings. At this stage, we used this already existing non-blind dataset with established baselines to build up momentum for researching the task. This dataset can be accessed through `http://cs.rochester.edu/nlp/rocstories/`.

As the training data, we released an extended set of ROCStories[2], called ROCStories Winter 2017. We followed the same crowdsourcing setup described in Mostafazadeh et al. Table 2 provides three example stories in this dataset. As these examples show, these are complete stories and do not come with a wrong ending[3]. Although we provided the additional ROCStories, the participants were encouraged to use or construct any training data of their choice. Overall, the participants were provided three datasets with the statistics listed in Table 3.

Following Mostafazadeh et al. (2016), we eval-

---

[2]The extended ROCStories dataset can be accessed via `http://cs.rochester.edu/nlp/rocstories/`.

[3]The ROCStories corpus can be used for a variety of applications ranging from story generation to script learning.

ROCStories (training data)	**98,159**
Story Cloze validation set, Spring 2016	**1,871**
Story Cloze test set, Spring 2016	**1,871**

Table 3: The size of the provided shared task datasets.

uate the systems in terms of accuracy, which we measure as $\frac{\#correct}{\#test\ cases}$. Any other details regarding our shared task can be accessed via our shared task page `http://cs.rochester.edu/nlp/rocstories/LSDSem17/`.

4 Submissions

The Shared Task was conducted through CodaLab competitions[4]. We received a total of 18 registrations, out of which eight teams participated: four teams from the US, three teams from Germany and one team from India.

In the following, we provide short paragraphs summarizing our baseline and approaches of the submissions. More details can be found in the respective system description papers.

msap (University of Washington). Linear classifier based on language modeling probabilities of the entire story, and linguistic features of only the ending sentences (Schwartz et al., 2017). These ending "style" features include sentence length as well as word and character n-gram in each candidate ending (independent of story). These style features have been shown useful in other tasks such as age, gender, or native language detection.

cogcomp (University of Illinois). Linear classification system that measures a story's coherence based on the sequence of events, emotional trajectory, and plot consistency. This model takes into account frame-based and sentiment-based language modeling probabilities as well as a topical consistency score.

acoli (Goethe University Frankfurt am Main) and **tbmihaylov (Heidelberg University).** Two resource-lean approaches that only make use of pretrained word representations and compositions thereof (Schenk and Chiarcos, 2017; Mihaylov and Frank, 2017). Composition functions are learned as part of a feed-forward and LSTM neural networks, respectively.

---

[4]The Story Cloze CodaLab page can be accessed here: `https://competitions.codalab.org/competitions/15333`

ukp (Technical University of Darmstadt). Combination of a neural network-based (Bi-LSTM) classifier and a traditional feature-rich approach (Bugert et al., 2017). Linguistic features include aspects of sentiment, negation, pronominalization and n-gram overlap between the story and possible endings.

roemmele (University of Southern California). Binary classifier based on a recurrent neural network that operates over (sentence-level) Skip-thought embeddings (Roemmele et al., 2017). For training, different data augmentation methods are explored.

mflor (Educational Testing Service). Rule-based combination of two systems that score possible endings in terms of how well they lexically cohere with and fit the sentiment of the given story (Flor and Somasundaran, 2017). Sentiment is given priority, and the model backs off to lexical coherence based on pointwise mutual information scores.

Pranav_Goel (IIT Varanasi). Ensemble model that takes into account scores from two systems that measure overlap in sentiment and sentence similarity between the story and the two possible endings (Goel and Singh, 2017).

ROCNLP (baseline) Two feed-forward neural networks trained jointly on ROCStories to project the four-sentences context and the right fifth sentence into the same vector space. This model is called Deep Structured Semantic Model (DSSM) (Huang et al., 2013) and had outperformed all the other baselines reported in Mostafazadeh et al. (2016).

5 Results

An overview of the models and the resources used in each participating system, along with their quantative results, is given in Table 4. Given that the DSSM model was previously trained on about 50K ROCStories, we retrained this model on our full dataset of 98,159 stories. We include the results of this model under ROCNLP in Table 4. With accuracy values in a range from 60% to 75.2%, we observe that all teams outperform the baseline model. The best result in this shared task has been achieved by **msap**, the participating team from the University of Washington.

Rank	CodaLab Id	Model	ROCStories	Pre-trained Embeddings	Other Resources	Accuracy
1	**msap**	Logistic regression	Spring 2016, Winter 2017	–	NLTK Tokenizer, Spacy POS tagger	**0.752**
2	**cogcomp**	Logistic regression	Spring 2016, Winter 2017	Word2Vec	UIUC NLP pipeline, FrameNet, two sentiment lexicons	0.744
3	**tbmihaylov**	LSTM	–	Word2Vec	–	0.728
4	**ukp**	BiLSTM	Spring 2016, Winter 2017	GloVe	Stanford CoreNLP, DKPro TC	0.717
5	**acoli**	SVM	–	GloVe, Word2Vec	–	0.700
6	**roemmele**	RNN	Spring 2016, Winter 2017	Skip-Thought	–	0.672
7	**mflor**	Rule-based	–	–	VADER sentiment lexicon, Gigaword corpus PMI scores	0.621
8	**Pranav_Goel**	Logistic regression	Spring 2016, Winter 2017	Word2Vec	VADER sentiment lexicon, SICK data set	0.604
9	**ROCNLP (baseline)**	DSSM	Spring 2016, Winter 2017	–	–	0.595

Table 4: Overview of models and resources used by the participating teams. For each team only their best performing system on the Spring 2016 Test Set is included, as submitted to CodaLab. Please refer to the system description papers for a list of other models. Human is reported to perform at 100%.

6 Discussion

We briefly highlight some observations regarding modeling choices and results.

Embeddings. All but two teams made use of pretrained embeddings for words or sentences. **tbmihaylov** (Mihaylov and Frank, 2017) experimented with various pretrained embeddings in their resource-lean model and found that the choice of embeddings has a considerable impact on model accuracy. Interestingly, the best participating team used no pretrained embeddings at all.

Neural networks. The six highest scoring models all include neural network architectures in one way or another. While the teams ranked 3–6 attempt to utilize hidden layers directly for prediction, the top two teams use the output of neural language models to generate different combinations of features. Further, while the third place team's best model was an LSTM, their logistic regression classifier with Word2Vec-based features achieved similar performance. The combination of different neural features (including non-neural ones) appears to have made the difference in the top system's ablation tests.

Sentiment. Three teams report concurrently that a sentiment model alone can achieve 60–65% accuracy but performance seems to vary dependent on implementation details. This is notable in that the sentiment baseline which chose the ending with a matching sentiment to the context (presented in Mostafazadeh et al. (2016)) did not achieve accuracy above random chance. One difference is that these more successful approaches used sentiment lexicons to score words and sentences, whereas Mostafazadeh et al. used the automatic sentiment classifier in Stanford's CoreNLP. Finally, **mflor** (Flor and Somasundaran, 2017) analyzed the Story Cloze Test Validation (Spring 2016) set and found that 78% of the stories have sentiment bearing words in the first sentences and in at least one possible ending. Evaluating on that subset showed increased performance, further suggesting that sentiment is an important factor in alternate ending prediction.

Stylistic Features on Endings. One of the models proposed by **msap** (Schwartz et al., 2017) ignored the entire story, building features only from the ending sentences. They trained a linear classifier on the right and wrong ending sentences adopting style features that have been shown useful in other tasks such as gender or native language detection. This model achieved remarkably good performance at 72.4%, indicating that there are characteristics inherent to right/wrong endings independent of story reasoning. It is not clear whether these results generalize to novel story ending predictions, beyond the particular Spring 2016 sets. Whether this model captures an artifact of the test set creation, or it indicates general features about how stories are ended must remain for future investigation.

Negative results. Some papers describe additional experiments with features and methods that are not part of the submitted system, because their inclusion resulted in sub-optimal performance. For example, **Pranav_Goel** (Goel and Singh, 2017) discuss additional similarity measures based on doc2vec sentence representations (Le and Mikolov, 2014); **tbmihaylov** (Mihaylov and Frank, 2017) experiment with ConceptNet Numberbatch embeddings (Speer and Chin, 2016); and **mflor** (Flor and Somasundaran, 2017) showcase results with alternative sentiment dictionaries such as MPQA (Wilson ct al., 2005).

7 Conclusions

All participants in the Story Cloze shared task of LSDSem outperformed the previously published best result of 58.5%, and the new state-of-the-art accuracy dramatically increased to 75.2% with the help of a well-designed RNNLM and unique stylistic features on the ending sentences.

One of the main takeaways from the 8 submissions is that the detection of correct ending sentences requires a variety of different reasoners. It appears from both results and post-analysis that sentiment is one factor in correct detection. However, it is also clear that coherence is critical, as the systems with language models all observed increases in prediction accuracy. Beyond these, the best performing system showed that there are stylistic features isolated in the ending sentences, suggesting yet another area of further investigation for the next phases of this task.

As the first shared task on SCT, we decided not to hold a blind challenge. For the future blind challenges, the question is how robust are the presented approaches to novel test cases and how well can they generalize out of the scope of the current evaluation sets. We speculate that the models which use generic language understanding and semantic cohesion criteria rather than relying on certain intricacies of the testing corpora can generalize more successfully, which should be carefully assessed in future.

Although this shared task was successful at setting a new state-of-the-art for SCT, clearly, there is still a long way towards achieving human-level performance of 100% on even the current test set. We are encouraged by the high level of participation in the LSDSem 2017 shared task, and hope the new models and results encourage further research in story understanding. Our findings can help direct the creation of the next SCT datasets towards enforcing deeper story understanding.

Acknowledgment

We would like to thank the wonderful crowd workers whose daily story writing made collecting the additional dataset possible. We thank Alyson Grealish and Ahmed Hassan Awadallah for their help in the quality control of ROCStories corpus. This work was supported in part by grant W911NF-15-1-0542 with the US Defense Advanced Research Projects Agency (DARPA) as a part of the Communicating with Computers (CwC) program, a grant from the Office of Naval Research, Army Research Office (ARO), and a DFG Research Fellowship (RO 4848/1-1).

References

Michael Bugert, Yevgeniy Puzikov, Andreas Rckl, Judith Eckle-Kohler, Teresa Martin, Eugenio Martnez-Cmara, Daniil Sorokin, Maxime Peyrard, and Iryna Gurevych. 2017. LSDSem 2017: Exploring data generation methods for the story cloze test. In *Proceedings of the 2nd Workshop on Linking Models of Lexical, Sentential and Discourse-level Semantics (LSDSem)*, Valencia, Spain. Association for Computational Linguistics.

Eugene Charniak. 1972. *Toward a Model of Children's Story Comprehension*. Ph.D. thesis, MIT.

Michael Flor and Swapna Somasundaran. 2017. Sentiment analysis and lexical cohesion for the story cloze task. In *Proceedings of the 2nd Workshop on Linking Models of Lexical, Sentential and Discourse-level Semantics (LSDSem)*, Valencia, Spain. Association for Computational Linguistics.

Pranav Goel and Anil Kumar Singh. 2017. IIT (BHU): System description for LSDSem'17. In *Proceedings of the 2nd Workshop on Linking Models of Lexical, Sentential and Discourse-level Semantics (LSDSem)*, Valencia, Spain. Association for Computational Linguistics.

Po-Sen Huang, Xiaodong He, Jianfeng Gao, Li Deng, Alex Acero, and Larry Heck. 2013. Learning deep structured semantic models for web search using clickthrough data. In *Proceedings of the 22nd ACM International Conference on Information & Knowledge Management*, (CIKM '13), pages 2333–2338, New York, NY, USA. ACM.

Quoc V Le and Tomas Mikolov. 2014. Distributed representations of sentences and documents. In *Proceedings of the 31st International Conference on Machine Learning*, Beijing, China.

Todor Mihaylov and Anette Frank. 2017. Simple story ending selection baselines. In *Proceedings of the 2nd Workshop on Linking Models of Lexical, Sentential and Discourse-level Semantics (LSDSem)*, Valencia, Spain. Association for Computational Linguistics.

Nasrin Mostafazadeh, Nathanael Chambers, Xiaodong He, Devi Parikh, Dhruv Batra, Lucy Vanderwende, Pushmeet Kohli, and James Allen. 2016. A corpus and cloze evaluation for deeper understanding of commonsense stories. In *Proceedings of the 2016 Conference of the North American Chapter of the Association for Computational Linguistics: Human Language Technologies*, pages 839–849, San Diego, California, June. Association for Computational Linguistics.

Melissa Roemmele, Sosuke Kobayashi, Naoya Inoue, and Andrew Gordon. 2017. An RNN-based binary classifier for the story cloze test. In *Proceedings of the 2nd Workshop on Linking Models of Lexical, Sentential and Discourse-level Semantics (LSDSem)*, Valencia, Spain. Association for Computational Linguistics.

Niko Schenk and Christian Chiarcos. 2017. Resource-lean modeling of coherence in commonsense stories. In *Proceedings of the 2nd Workshop on Linking Models of Lexical, Sentential and Discourse-level Semantics (LSDSem)*, Valencia, Spain. Association for Computational Linguistics.

Lenhart K. Schubert and Chung Hee Hwang. 2000. Episodic logic meets little red riding hood: A comprehensive, natural representation for language understanding. In *Natural Language Processing and Knowledge Representation: Language for Knowledge and Knowledge for Language*. MIT/AAAI Press.

Roy Schwartz, Maarten Sap, Ioannis Konstas, Leila Zilles, Yejin Choi, and Noah A. Smith. 2017. Story cloze task: UW NLP system. In *Proceedings of the 2nd Workshop on Linking Models of Lexical, Sentential and Discourse-level Semantics (LSDSem)*, Valencia, Spain. Association for Computational Linguistics.

Robert Speer and Joshua Chin. 2016. An ensemble method to produce high-quality word embeddings. *arXiv preprint arXiv:1604.01692.*

Scott R. Turner. 1994. The creative process: A computer model of storytelling and creativity. *Hillsdale: Lawrence Erlbaum.*

Theresa Wilson, Janyce Wiebe, and Paul Hoffmann. 2005. Recognizing contextual polarity in phrase-level sentiment analysis. In *Proceedings of Human Language Technology Conference and Conference on Empirical Methods in Natural Language Processing*, pages 347–354, Vancouver, British Columbia, Canada, October.

Terry Winograd. 1972. *Understanding Natural Language.* Academic Press, Inc., Orlando, FL, USA.

Story Cloze Task: UW NLP System

Roy Schwartz[1,2], Maarten Sap[1], Ioannis Konstas[1],
Leila Zilles[1], Yejin Choi[1] and Noah A. Smith[1]

[1]Computer Science & Engineering, University of Washington, Seattle, WA 98195, USA
[2]Allen Institute for Artificial Intelligence, Seattle, WA 98103, USA
{roysch,msap,ikonstas,lzilles,yejin,nasmith}@cs.washington.edu

Abstract

This paper describes University of Washington NLP's submission for the Linking Models of Lexical, Sentential and Discourse-level Semantics (LSDSem 2017) shared task—the *Story Cloze Task*. Our system is a linear classifier with a variety of features, including both the scores of a neural language model and style features. We report 75.2% accuracy on the task. A further discussion of our results can be found in Schwartz et al. (2017).

Story Prefix	Ending
Kathy went shopping. She found a pair of great shoes. The shoes were $300. She bought the shoes.	She felt buyer's remorse after the purchase.
	Kathy hated buying shoes.

Table 1: Examples of stories from the story cloze task (Mostafazadeh et al., 2016). The left column shows that first four sentences of a story. The right column shows two contrastive endings for the story: a coherent ending (upper row) and a incoherent one (bottom row).

1 Introduction

As an effort to advance commonsense understanding, Mostafazadeh et al. (2016) developed the *story cloze task*, which is the focus of the LSDSem 2017 shared task. In this task, systems are given two short, self-contained stories, which differ only in their last sentence: one has a *right* (coherent) ending, and the other has a *wrong* (incoherent) ending. The task is to tell which is the *right* story. In addition to the task, the authors also introduced the *ROC story corpus*—a training corpus of five-sentence (coherent) stories. Table 1 shows an example of a *coherent* story and an *incoherent* story from the story cloze task.

In this paper, we describe University of Washington NLP's submission for the shared task. Our system explores several types of features for the task. First, we train a neural language model (Mikolov et al., 2010) on the ROC story corpus. We use the probabilities assigned by the model to each of the endings (*right* and *wrong*) as classification features.

Second, we attempt to distinguish between *right* and *wrong* endings using style features, such as sentence length, character *n*-grams and word *n*-grams. Our intuition is that the *right* endings use a different style compared to the *wrong* endings. The features we use were shown useful for style detection in tasks such as age (Schler et al., 2006), gender (Argamon et al., 2003), and authorship profiling (Stamatatos, 2009).

We feed our features to a logistic regression classifier, and evaluate our system on the shared task. Our system obtains 75.2% accuracy on the test set. Our findings hint that the different writing tasks used to create the story cloze task—writing *right* and *wrong* endings—impose different writing styles on authors. This is further discussed in Schwartz et al. (2017).

2 System Description

We design a system that predicts, given a pair of story endings, which is the *right* one and which is the *wrong* one. Our system applies a linear classifier guided by several types of features to solve the task. We describe the system in detail below.

Proceedings of the 2nd Workshop on Linking Models of Lexical, Sentential and Discourse-level Semantics, pages 52–55,
Valencia, Spain, April 3, 2017. ©2017 Association for Computational Linguistics

2.1 Model

We train a binary logistic regression classifier to distinguish between *right* and *wrong* stories. We use the set of *right* stories as positive samples and the set of *wrong* stories as negative samples. At test time, for a given pair, we consider the classification results of both candidates. If our classifier assigns different labels to each candidate, we keep them. If not, the label whose posterior probability is lower is reversed. We describe the classification features below.

2.2 Features

We use two types of features, designed to capture different aspects of the problem. We use *neural language model* features to leverage corpus level word distributions, specifically longer term sequence probabilities. We use *stylistic* features to capture differences in writing between *coherent* story endings and *incoherent* ones.

Language model features. We experiment with state-of-the-art text comprehension models, specifically an LSTM (Hochreiter and Schmidhuber, 1997) recurrent neural network language model (RNNLM; Mikolov et al., 2010). Our RNNLM is used to generate two different probabilities: $p_\theta(\text{ending})$, which is the language model probability of the fifth sentence alone and $p_\theta(\text{ending} \mid \text{story})$, which is the RNNLM probability of the fifth sentence given the first four sentences. We use both of these probabilities as classification features.

In addition, we also apply a third feature:

$$\frac{p_\theta(\text{ending} \mid \text{story})}{p_\theta(\text{ending})} \tag{1}$$

The intuition is that a *correct* ending should be unsurprising (to the model) given the four preceding sentences of the story (the numerator), controlling for the inherent surprise of the words in that ending (the denominator).[1]

Stylistic features. We hypothesize that *right* and *wrong* endings might be distinguishable using style features. We adopt style features that have been shown useful in the past in tasks such as detection of age (Schler et al., 2006; Rosenthal and McKeown, 2011; Nguyen et al., 2011), gender (Argamon et al., 2003; Schler et al., 2006; Bamman et al., 2014), and native language (Koppel et al., 2005; Tsur and Rappoport, 2007; Bergsma et al., 2012).

We add the following classification features to capture style differences between the two endings. These features are computed on the story endings alone (*right* or *wrong*), and do not consider, either at train or at test time, the first four (shared) sentences of each story.

- **Length.** The number of words in the sentence.

- **Word *n*-grams.** We use sequences of 1–5 words. Following Tsur et al. (2010) and Schwartz et al. (2013), we distinguish between high frequency and low frequency words. Specifically, we replace content words, which are often low frequency, with their part-of-speech tags (Nouns, Verbs, Adjectives, and Adverbs).

- **Character *n*-grams.** Character *n*-grams are useful features in the detection of author style (Stamatatos, 2009) or language identification (Lui and Baldwin, 2011). We use character 4-grams.

2.3 Experimental Setup

The story cloze task doesn't have a training corpus for the *right* and *wrong* endings. Therefore, we use the development set as our training set, holding out 10% for development (3,366 training endings, 374 for development). We keep the story cloze test set as is (3,742 endings).

We use Python's sklearn logistic regression implementation with L_2 regularization, performing grid search on the development set to tune a single hyperparameter—the regularization parameter.

For computing the RNN features, we start by tokenizing the text using the nltk tokenizer.[2] We then use TensorFlow[3] to train the RNNLM using a single-layer LSTM of hidden dimension 512. We use the ROC Stories for training, setting aside 10% for validation of the language model.[4] We replace all words occurring less than 3 times by a special out-of-vocabulary character, yielding a vocabulary size of 21,582. Only during training, we apply a

---

[1] Note that taking the logarithm of the expression in Equation 1 gives the pointwise mutual information between the story and the ending, under the language model.

[2] `www.nltk.org/api/nltk.tokenize.html`
[3] `www.tensorflow.org`
[4] We train on both the Spring 2016 and the Winter 2017 datasets, a total of roughly 100K stories.

Model	Acc.
DSSM (Mostafazadeh et al., 2016)	0.585
LexVec (Salle et al., 2016)	0.599
RNNLM features	0.677
Stylistic features	0.724
Combined (Style + RNNLM)	**0.752**
Human judgment	1.000

Table 2: Results on the test set of the story cloze task. The first block are published results, the second block are our results. LexVec results are taken from (Speer et al., 2017). Human judgement scores are taken from (Mostafazadeh et al., 2016).

dropout rate of 60% while running the LSTM over all 5 sentences of the stories. Using Adam optimizer (Kingma and Ba, 2015) and a learning rate of $\eta = .001$, we train to minimize cross-entropy. The resulting RNN features (see Section 2.2) are taken in log space.

For the style features, we add a START symbol at the beginning of each sentence.[5] We keep n-gram (character or word) features that occur at least five times in the training set. All stylistic feature values are normalized to the range [0, 1]. For the part-of-speech features, we tag all endings with the Spacy POS tagger.[6] The total number of features used by our system is 7,651.

3 Results

The performance of our system is described in Table 2. With 75.2% accuracy, our system achieves 15.3% better than the published state of the art (Salle et al., 2016). The table also shows an analysis of the different features types used by our system. While our RNNLM features alone reach 67.7%, the style features perform better—72.4%. This suggests that while this task is about story understanding, there is some information contained in stylistic features, which are slightly less sensitive to content. As expected, the RNNLM features complement the stylistic ones, boosting performance by 7.5% (over the RNNLM features) and 2.8% (over the style features).

In an attempt to provide explanation to the strong performance of the stylistic feature, we hypothesize that the different writing tasks—writing a *right* and a *wrong* ending—impose a different style on the authors, which is expressed in the different style adopted in each of the cases. The reader is referred to Schwartz et al. (2017) for more details and discussion.

4 Conclusion

This paper described University of Washington NLP's submission to the LSDSem 2017 Shared Task. Our system leveraged both neural language model features and stylistic features, achieving 75.2% accuracy on the classification task.

Acknowledgments

The authors thank the shared task organizers and anonymous reviewers for feedback. This research was supported in part by DARPA under the Communicating with Computers program.

References

Shlomo Argamon, Moshe Koppel, Jonathan Fine, and Anat Rachel Shimoni. 2003. Gender, genre, and writing style in formal written texts. *Text*, 23(3):321–346.

David Bamman, Jacob Eisenstein, and Tyler Schnoebelen. 2014. Gender identity and lexical variation in social media. *Journal of Sociolinguistics*, 18(2):135–160.

Shane Bergsma, Matt Post, and David Yarowsky. 2012. Stylometric analysis of scientific articles. In *Proceedings of the 2012 Conference of the North American Chapter of the Association for Computational Linguistics: Human Language Technologies*, pages 327–337, Montréal, Canada, June. Association for Computational Linguistics.

Sepp Hochreiter and Jürgen Schmidhuber. 1997. Long short-term memory. *Neural Computation*, 9(8):1735–1780.

Diederik Kingma and Jimmy Ba. 2015. Adam: A method for stochastic optimization. In *Proceedings of the International Conference on Learning Representations*, San Diego, California, USA.

Moshe Koppel, Jonathan Schler, and Kfir Zigdon. 2005. Determining an author's native language by mining a text for errors. In *Proceedings of the Eleventh ACM SIGKDD International Conference on Knowledge Discovery in Data Mining*, pages 624–628, Chicago, Illinois, USA. Association for Computing Machinery.

Marco Lui and Timothy Baldwin. 2011. Cross-domain feature selection for language identification. In *Proceedings of 5th International Joint Conference on*

---

[5] Virtually all sentences end with a period or an exclamation mark, so we do not add a STOP symbol.

[6] `spacy.io/`

Natural Language Processing, pages 553–561, Chiang Mai, Thailand, November. Asian Federation of Natural Language Processing.

Tomáš Mikolov, Martin Karafiát, Lukáš Burget, Jan Černocký, and Sanjeev Khudanpur. 2010. Recurrent neural network based language model. In *Proceedings of the 11th Annual Conference of the International Speech Communication Association*, pages 1045–1048, Makuhari, Chiba, Japan. International Speech Communication Association.

Nasrin Mostafazadeh, Nathanael Chambers, Xiaodong He, Devi Parikh, Dhruv Batra, Lucy Vanderwende, Pushmeet Kohli, and James Allen. 2016. A corpus and cloze evaluation for deeper understanding of commonsense stories. In *Proceedings of the 2016 Conference of the North American Chapter of the Association for Computational Linguistics: Human Language Technologies*, pages 839–849, San Diego, California, USA, June. Association for Computational Linguistics.

Dong Nguyen, Noah A. Smith, and Carolyn P. Rosé. 2011. Author age prediction from text using linear regression. In *Proceedings of the 5th ACL-HLT Workshop on Language Technology for Cultural Heritage, Social Sciences, and Humanities*, pages 115–123, Portland, Oregon, USA, June. Association for Computational Linguistics.

Sara Rosenthal and Kathleen McKeown. 2011. Age prediction in blogs: A study of style, content, and online behavior in pre- and post-social media generations. In *Proceedings of the 49th Annual Meeting of the Association for Computational Linguistics: Human Language Technologies*, pages 763–772, Portland, Oregon, USA, June. Association for Computational Linguistics.

Alexandre Salle, Marco Idiart, and Aline Villavicencio. 2016. Enhancing the lexvec distributed word representation model using positional contexts and external memory. arXiv:1606.01283.

Jonathan Schler, Moshe Koppel, Shlomo Argamon, and James Pennebaker. 2006. Effects of age and gender on blogging. In *AAAI Spring Symposium: Computational Approaches to Analyzing Weblogs*, pages 199–205, Palo Alto, California, USA, March. AAAI Press.

Roy Schwartz, Oren Tsur, Ari Rappoport, and Moshe Koppel. 2013. Authorship attribution of micromessages. In *Proceedings of the 2013 Conference on Empirical Methods in Natural Language Processing*, pages 1880–1891, Seattle, Washington, USA, October. Association for Computational Linguistics.

Roy Schwartz, Maarten Sap, Ioannis Konstas, Leila Zilles, Yejin Choi, and Noah A. Smith. 2017. The effect of different writing tasks on linguistic style: A case study of the ROC story cloze task. arXiv:1702.01841.

Robert Speer, Joshua Chin, and Catherine Havasi. 2017. Conceptnet 5.5: An open multilingual graph of general knowledge. In *Proceedings of the 31st AAAI Conference on Artificial Intelligence*, San Francisco, California, USA, February. AAAI Press.

Efstathios Stamatatos. 2009. A survey of modern authorship attribution methods. *Journal of the American Society for information Science and Technology*, 60(3):538–556.

Oren Tsur and Ari Rappoport. 2007. Using classifier features for studying the effect of native language on the choice of written second language words. In *Proceedings of the Workshop on Cognitive Aspects of Computational Language Acquisition*, pages 9–16, Prague, Czech Republic, June. Association for Computational Linguistics.

Oren Tsur, Dmitry Davidov, and Ari Rappoport. 2010. ICWSM—a great catchy name: Semi-supervised recognition of sarcastic sentences in online product reviews. In *Proceedings of the Fourth International AAAI Conference on Weblogs and Social Media*, pages 162–169, Washington, DC, USA, May. AAAI Press.

LSDSem 2017: Exploring Data Generation Methods for the Story Cloze Test

Michael Bugert[*], Yevgeniy Puzikov[*], Andreas Rücklé[*],
Judith Eckle-Kohler[*], Teresa Martin[†], Eugenio Martínez-Cámara[*],
Daniil Sorokin[*], Maxime Peyrard[†] and Iryna Gurevych[*]

[*]Ubiquitous Knowledge Processing Lab (UKP-TUDA)
Department of Computer Science, Technische Universität Darmstadt
`www.ukp.tu-darmstadt.de`
[†]Research Training Group AIPHES
Department of Computer Science, Technische Universität Darmstadt
`www.aiphes.tu-darmstadt.de`

Abstract

The Story Cloze test (Mostafazadeh et al., 2016) is a recent effort in providing a common test scenario for text understanding systems. As part of the LSDSem 2017 shared task, we present a system based on a deep learning architecture combined with a rich set of manually-crafted linguistic features. The system outperforms all known baselines for the task, suggesting that the chosen approach is promising. We additionally present two methods for generating further training data based on stories from the ROCStories corpus. Our system and generated data are publicly available on GitHub[1].

1 Introduction

The goal of the Story Cloze test is to provide a common ground for the evaluation of systems on language understanding (Mostafazadeh et al., 2016). Given four sentences of a story on everyday life events, a system has to identify the correct ending from a set of two predefined ending sentences. The "correct" ending in this case is the one which most humans would choose as the closing sentence for the story context.

We first report the discoveries we made while exploring the provided datasets (Section 2) followed by a description of our system (Section 3). We present and discuss its results (Sections 4 and 5) and come to a close in the conclusion (Section 6).

2 Dataset Exploration

Mostafazadeh et al. (2016) provide a validation and

a test set for the Story Cloze test, both of which contain around 1800 stories[2]. Each of those stories consists of four context sentences and two endings to choose from. Additionally, two *ROCStories* datasets were made available with close to 100 000 stories in total. Stories from these datasets also cover everyday life events but consist of a fixed number of five sentences without ending candidates.

To gain an overview of the task, we categorized two hundred stories from the validation set based on how their correct ending can be identified.

We noticed that a large set of stories can indeed be solved via text understanding and logical inference. This includes stories where the correct ending is more likely according to script knowledge[3] (Schank and Abelson, 1977), where the topic of the wrong ending doesn't match the story context[4] or where the wrong ending contradicts the story context[5].

For some stories, the correct ending cannot be identified rationally, but rather according to commonly accepted moral values[6] or based on the reader's expectation of a positive mood in a story[7]. Regarding sentiments, we generally noticed a bias towards stories with "happy endings", i. e. stories where the sentiment expressed in the correct ending is more positive than for the wrong ending.

We infer from these observations that an approach focusing exclusively on text understanding

---

[1]github.com/UKPLab/lsdsem2017-story-cloze

[2]As of Feb. 2017, see cs.rochester.edu/nlp/rocstories
[3]See story 52dbbfda-5b42-4ace-8d59-55cee3eb30c0 in the Story Cloze validation set.
[4]See f8ff777f-de4d-4e3a-91bd-b197ed13f78e ibid.
[5]See a11cf506-7d19-4ab9-b0ac-a0fd85a9bd38 ibid.
[6]See 195a43c7-d43e-48e4-845b-fd6c75609df2 ibid.
[7]See 80b6447f-4c37-4194-9862-3785e5075463 ibid.

Proceedings of the 2nd Workshop on Linking Models of Lexical, Sentential and Discourse-level Semantics, pages 56–61,
Valencia, Spain, April 3, 2017. ©2017 Association for Computational Linguistics

should perform well. However, the dataset suggests that an approach which (additionally) exploits how humans write and perceive stories could also lead to respectable results, albeit not in the way originally intended for the Story Cloze test.

3 System Description

We interpret the Story Cloze test as a fully supervised learning problem, meaning we train and test our approach on instances consisting of four context sentences and two ending candidates (i. e. the format of the Story Cloze datasets). This stands in contrast to the systems reported by Mostafazadeh et al. (2016) which were trained on five-sentence stories (the ROCStories dataset).

Our approach builds around recent advances of deep learning methods and conventional feature engineering techniques.

The core of the system is a Bidirectional Recurrent Neural Network (BiRNN) (Schuster and Paliwal, 1997) with Long Short-Term Memory (LSTM) units (Hochreiter and Schmidhuber, 1997), which computes a feature representation of all given sentences. This representation is enriched by feature vectors computed over both ending candidates. To predict the correct ending of a story, we execute our neural network twice to obtain a score for each ending. These scores are compared to make a final decision. The feature vectors ensure that information on the respective other ending is available to the network during both executions.

Note that we could have instead learned ending embeddings jointly by feeding the network with both endings at the same time. In order to train a network to distinguish between correct and wrong endings, we would have had to feed the same pair another time, but with the endings swapped and the label set to its binary counterpart. However, we were concerned that such a system would eventually learn the position of the correct ending instead of its meaning. Hence, we decided against such a joint learning approach.

The following sections cover the features and neural network architecture in greater detail.

3.1 Features

We defined a set of linguistic features in order to profit from the discoveries of our dataset exploration (see Section 2). The features are:

NGramOverlap: The number of overlapping n-grams between an ending and a story context

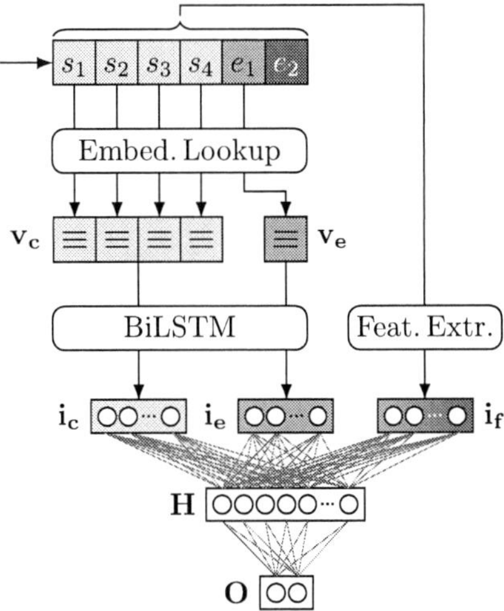

Figure 1: Neural network architecture. Depicted is the execution for obtaining a score for ending e_1.

for $n = \{1, 2, 3\}$. We filtered out bigrams and trigrams using a linguistically motivated list of stopwords.

EndingLength: The token count of an ending.

Negation: The presence of words indicating negation (*none*, *never*, etc.) in an ending.

PronounContrast: The presence of pronoun mismatches between a story context and an ending. This helps to detect cases where the wrong ending is written in first person although the story context is written in third person.

SentiContrast: Disagreement in the sentiment value between the third and fourth sentences of a context and an ending. The sentiment value was computed based on a sentiment word list manually extracted from the ROCStories dataset.

For each of the features listed above, an additional feature was added to model the feature value difference between the two endings of a story. All features were extracted using the DKPro TC Framework (Daxenberger et al., 2014).

3.2 Neural Network

The overall architecture of our neural network model is shown in Figure 1.

First, the tokens of the context sentences $s_1, \ldots, s_4$ and of ending e_1 are looked up in the word embedding matrix to obtain vectorized representations. The embeddings of the context sentences are concatenated into the vector $\mathbf{v_c}$, whereas those of the ending form vector $\mathbf{v_e}$. $\mathbf{v_c}$ and $\mathbf{v_e}$ are fed separately to a pair of RNN networks (forward and backward) with LSTM units. This BiLSTM module encodes the meaning of context and ending in two separate vectors, $\mathbf{i_c}$ and $\mathbf{i_e}$. Given the vector of feature values $\mathbf{i_f}$, extracted externally on the four context sentences and both endings, we concatenate $\mathbf{i_c}$, $\mathbf{i_e}$ and $\mathbf{i_f}$ and feed them to the dense hidden layer $\mathbf{H}$. The output of $\mathbf{H}$ is fed to the output layer, $\mathbf{O}$. Afterwards, the softmax function is applied on the output of $\mathbf{O}$ to obtain a score representing the probability of ending e_1 being correct.

The same procedure is applied for ending e_2 in place of ending e_1. Then, the highest-scoring ending is chosen as the correct ending of the story.

Due to time constraints and system complexity we decided against hyper-parameter optimization and chose parameter values we deemed reasonable: We used pretrained 100-dimensional GloVe embeddings (Pennington et al., 2014)[8]. Following previous work on using BiLSTMs in NLP tasks (Tan et al., 2015; Tan et al., 2016; dos Santos et al., 2016), we chose a dimensionality of 141 for the LSTM output vectors and hidden layer $\mathbf{H}$.

We employ zero padding for sentences longer than 20 tokens. The network was trained in batches (size 40) for 30 epochs with the Adam optimizer (Kingma and Ba, 2014), starting with a learning rate of 10^{-4}. We apply dropout ($p = 0.3$) after computing the BiLSTM output. Finally, ReLu (Glorot et al., 2011) is used as an activation function in layer $\mathbf{H}$. The system was implemented using the TensorFlow library (Abadi et al., 2016).

3.3 Intermediate Results

We performed an intermediate evaluation of the previously described system on the Story Cloze validation set. To this end, we partitioned the dataset into a training and development split (85 % and 15 %, respectively). We compared the following systems:

BiLSTM-V: Our proposed system, trained on the 85 % training split without making use of the feature set described in Section 3.1.

BiLSTM-VF: Same as BiLSTM-V, but including the feature set.

Happy: Motivated by our dataset exploration, this baseline always picks the happier ending (the ending with the more positive sentiment). We

employed the state-of-the-art sentiment annotator by Socher et al. (2013) for this purpose. This system does not take the story context into account.

The happy ending baseline reached an accuracy of 0.616 on the development split which is substantially higher than random guessing. BiLSTM-V scored 0.708 whereas BiLSTM-VF reached a slightly higher accuracy of 0.712.

3.4 Dataset Augmentation

Because our presented approach conducts supervised learning, it requires training data in the same form as testing data. Up to this point, the only dataset available in this form is the Story Cloze validation set which consists of comparably few instances for training. We experimented with ways to automatically create larger training datasets.

3.4.1 Related Work in Data Augmentation

Methods for automatic training data augmentation using unlabeled data are investigated in semi-supervised learning and have been successfully applied in many NLP tasks, for example in word sense disambiguation (Pham et al., 2005), semantic role labeling (Fürstenau and Lapata, 2012; Woodsend and Lapata, 2014) and textual entailment (Zanzotto and Pennacchiotti, 2010). Another example, which is similar to the Story Cloze test, is the task of selecting the correct answer to a question from a pool of answer candidates. To train models for this task, Feng et al. (2015) have extended a corpus of question-answer pairs by automatically adding negative answers to each pair.

We draw our inspiration from the aforementioned work and propose two methods for augmenting the ROCStories dataset in order to use it for supervised learning.

3.4.2 Shuffling

Given a ROCStory, shuffle the four context sentences, then randomly swap the fifth sentence with one of the first four. The resulting story is perceived as wrong by humans since the shuffling breaks causal and temporal relationships between the sentences. This method resembles the data quality evaluation conducted by Mostafazadeh et al. (2016).

3.4.3 KDE Sampling

In order to obtain a dataset of the same structure as the Story Cloze datasets, we heuristically complement each ROCStory with a wrong ending taken

---

[8]nlp.stanford.edu/data/glove.6B.zip

Story ID	Story Context	Correct Ending	Gen. Wrong Ending
3447901e-6f57 -4810-9d3c -92d72b6c0b42	A swan swam gracefully through the water. It was beautiful and white. It had a long orange beak. The crowd gathered and observed it.	It was a beautiful creature.	A large blue whale breached the water before Kathy's eyes.
0dd3e2c3-3ea4 -450a-97c4 -42a54c426018	Jane had recently gotten a new job. She was nervous about her first day of work. On the first day of work, Jane overslept. Jane arrived at work an hour late.	Jane did not make a good impression at her new job.	She told her husband that she was going all out this year.

Table 1: ROCStories with wrong endings as generated by the KDE sampling technique

from a pool of sentences. The pool can be chosen arbitrarily but for the sake of simplicity, we decided to use the existing set of ROCStory endings themselves.

Given four ROCStory context sentences, we measure the similarity between this context and each sentence from the pool (excluding the original ending). To ensure that endings match the topic and narrative of their context, our similarity measure is based on word embeddings of content words and a bag-of-words vector of occurring pronouns.

Instead of directly choosing whichever ending sentence scores the highest similarity, we attempt to replicate the characteristics of the Story Cloze datasets as close as possible. Therefore, we observe the distribution of similarity values present between each story context and its wrong ending in the validation set. Using kernel density estimation, we obtain the probability density function (PDF) of these similarity values.

To choose an ending for a ROCStory context, we then sample a similarity value from this PDF and identify the sentence in the pool whose similarity is closest to the sampled value. In a final step, we replace proper nouns occurring in the ending sentence with random proper nouns from the story context, based on POS-tags.

Table 1 shows two exemplary story endings generated using this method.

3.4.4 Comparison

We constructed two training datasets, one for each of the two augmentation methods. We then trained our BiLSTM approach (without features) for each dataset and compared their performance on the full Story Cloze validation set. The BiLSTM using the shuffled ROCStories reached an accuracy of 0.615, compared to the one using the KDE sampling method with 0.630.

From looking at the accuracies, the difference in quality between the two methods is slim. However, the quality of the shuffled stories is inferior to those of the KDE sampling method from a human

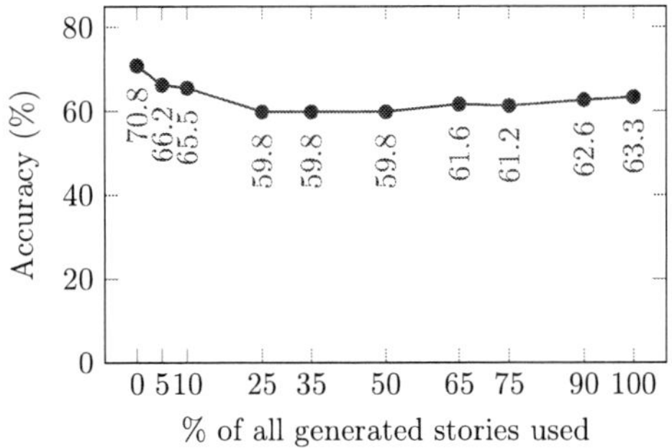

Figure 2: Accuracies on the validation set development split for BiLSTM systems trained on the training split plus a varying amount of all 98 166 generated stories.

point of view. For this reason, we conduct all subsequent data augmentation experiments using the KDE sampling method.

4 Results

Following our motivation for data augmentation, we trained several BiLSTM systems on the training split of the Story Cloze validation set, augmented by a varying amount of stories generated by KDE sampling. Figure 2 shows the accuracy of these systems evaluated on the 15 % development split of the validation set. As can be seen, in all our experiments with augmentation there occurs a decrease in performance compared to the results of BiLSTM-V/BiLSTM-VF on the same data (see Section 3.3). We discuss possible reasons for this result in Section 5.

For the final evaluation, we compare the following approaches:

DSSM: The best performing baseline reported by Mostafazadeh et al. (2016).

Happy, BiLSTM-V, BiLSTM-VF: The systems previously explained in Section 3.3.

BiLSTM-T: To assess the quality of the KDE sampling method in isolation, we also include a BiLSTM system in the evaluation which is trained only on the ROCStories corpus with

Approach	Validation		Test
	Dev	Full	
DSSM	–	0.604	0.585
Happy	0.616	0.590	0.602
BiLSTM-V	0.708	–	0.701[*]
BiLSTM-VF	0.712	–	**0.717**[*]
BiLSTM-T	0.637	–	0.560
BiLSTM-TF	0.634	–	0.584

Table 2: System accuracies on the Story Cloze datasets. Results marked by * are statistically significant according to McNemar's test with a *p-value* ≤ 0.05.

generated wrong endings.

BiLSTM-TF: Same as BiLSTM-T, but including the feature set.

Table 2 shows the performance of the systems on the Story Cloze test set and (if applicable) on the full validation set or its development split. It can be seen that our happy ending baseline performs comparably to the more elaborate DSSM baseline. BiLSTM-V/VF outperform the two baselines significantly. BiLSTM-T/TF fall short in accuracy compared to the ones trained on the validation set alone. The addition of features leads to improvements except for BiLSTM-T/TF when evaluated on the development split of the validation set.

5 Discussion

We manually examined several stories which were misclassified by BiLSTM-VF to identify its weaknesses. In the majority of cases, misclassified stories were sparse in sentiment or relied heavily on logical inference for identifying the correct ending. This appears plausible to us, since neither the BiLSTM nor the feature set were explicitly designed to perform advanced logical inference.

The proposed features increase the performance of our BiLSTM system. The data properties they capture are different from the distributional similarities of word embeddings and thus serve as an additional supervising signal for the neural network.

Given Figure 2 and the disparity between the results of BiLSTM-T/TF and BiLSTM-V/VF, we have to conclude that the training data augmentation did not work as well as we expected.

While the KDE sampling method creates stories resembling the ones found in the Story Cloze

validation and test datasets, it does not reproduce the characteristics of these original stories well enough to produce truly valuable training data. As an example, the method does not take sentiment into account, although we demonstrated that the Story Cloze datasets are biased towards happy endings. Incorporating further characteristics into the method would amount to redefining the utilized similarity measure (no modifications would be necessary for the core idea of sampling a probability distribution).

6 Conclusion

We showed that using a sentiment-based baseline, it is trivial to reach 60 % accuracy on the Story Cloze test set without relying on text understanding. However, more sophisticated techniques are required for reaching better results. Using a deep learning architecture enriched with a set of linguistically motivated features, we surpass all previously published baselines on the task and reach 71.7% accuracy on the test set.

We proposed two methods which generate additional training data for conducting supervised learning on the Story Cloze test. To our surprise, the systems trained on generated training data performed worse than those trained on conventional training data. This could be due to our data generation not reproducing the characteristics of the original Story Cloze datasets well enough. Nonetheless, we consider the presented methods to be a valuable contribution related to the task.

Acknowledgments

We thank the anonymous reviewers for their valuable comments and insights.

This work has been supported by the German Research Foundation as part of the Research Training Group "Adaptive Preparation of Information from Heterogeneous Sources" (AIPHES) under grant No. GRK 1994/1, as part of the German-Israeli Project Cooperation (DIP, grant No. DA 1600/1-1 and grant No. GU 798/17-1), and as part of the QA-EduInf project (grant No. GU 798/18-1 and grant No. RI 803/12-1).

References

Martín Abadi, Paul Barham, Jianmin Chen, Zhifeng Chen, Andy Davis, Jeffrey Dean, Matthieu Devin, Sanjay Ghemawat, Geoffrey Irving, Michael Isard, Manjunath Kudlur, Josh Levenberg, Rajat Monga,

Sherry Moore, Derek G. Murray, Benoit Steiner, Paul Tucker, Vijay Vasudevan, Pete Warden, Martin Wicke, Yuan Yu, and Xiaoqiang Zheng. 2016. TensorFlow: A System for Large-Scale Machine Learning. In *12th USENIX Symposium on Operating Systems Design and Implementation (OSDI 16)*, pages 265–283, GA. USENIX Association.

Johannes Daxenberger, Oliver Ferschke, Iryna Gurevych, and Torsten Zesch. 2014. DKPro TC: A Java-based Framework for Supervised Learning Experiments on Textual Data. In *Proceedings of 52nd Annual Meeting of the Association for Computational Linguistics: System Demonstrations*, pages 61–66. Association for Computational Linguistics.

Cícero Nogueira dos Santos, Ming Tan, Bing Xiang, and Bowen Zhou. 2016. Attentive Pooling Networks. *CoRR*, abs/1602.03609.

Minwei Feng, Bing Xiang, Michael R. Glass, Lidan Wang, and Bowen Zhou. 2015. Applying deep learning to answer selection: A study and an open task. In *2015 IEEE Workshop on Automatic Speech Recognition and Understanding (ASRU)*, pages 813–820.

Hagen Fürstenau and Mirella Lapata. 2012. Semi-Supervised Semantic Role Labeling via Structural Alignment. *Computational Linguistics*, 38:135–171.

Xavier Glorot, Antoine Bordes, and Yoshua Bengio. 2011. Deep sparse rectifier neural networks. In *AISTATS*, volume 15, page 275.

Sepp Hochreiter and Jürgen Schmidhuber. 1997. Long Short-Term Memory. *Neural Computation*, 9:1735–1780.

Diederik P. Kingma and Jimmy Ba. 2014. Adam: A Method for Stochastic Optimization. *CoRR*, abs/1412.6980.

Nasrin Mostafazadeh, Nathanael Chambers, Xiaodong He, Devi Parikh, Dhruv Batra, Lucy Vanderwende, Pushmeet Kohli, and James Allen. 2016. A Corpus and Cloze Evaluation for Deeper Understanding of Commonsense Stories. In *Proceedings of the 2016 Conference of the North American Chapter of the Association for Computational Linguistics: Human Language Technologies*, pages 839–849, San Diego, California. Association for Computational Linguistics.

Jeffrey Pennington, Richard Socher, and Christopher Manning. 2014. GloVe: Global Vectors for Word Representation. In *Proceedings of the 2014 Conference on Empirical Methods in Natural Language Processing (EMNLP)*, pages 1532–1543, Doha, Qatar. Association for Computational Linguistics.

Thanh Phong Pham, Hwee Tou Ng, and Wee Sun Lee. 2005. Word Sense Disambiguation with Semi-supervised Learning. In *Proceedings of the 20th National Conference on Artificial Intelligence - Volume 3*, AAAI'05, pages 1093–1098, Pittsburgh, Pennsylvania. AAAI Press.

Roger C. Schank and Robert P. Abelson. 1977. *Scripts, Plans, Goals, and Understanding: An Inquiry Into Human Knowledge Structures*. The Artificial Intelligence Series. Lawrence Erlbaum Associates.

Mike Schuster and Kuldip K. Paliwal. 1997. Bidirectional recurrent neural networks. *IEEE Trans. Signal Processing*, 45:2673–2681.

Richard Socher, Alex Perelygin, Jean Wu, Jason Chuang, Christopher D. Manning, Andrew Ng, and Christopher Potts. 2013. Recursive Deep Models for Semantic Compositionality Over a Sentiment Treebank. In *Proceedings of the 2013 Conference on Empirical Methods in Natural Language Processing*, pages 1631–1642, Seattle, Washington, USA. Association for Computational Linguistics.

Ming Tan, Bing Xiang, and Bowen Zhou. 2015. LSTM-based Deep Learning Models for non-factoid answer selection. *CoRR*, abs/1511.04108.

Ming Tan, Cicero dos Santos, Bing Xiang, and Bowen Zhou. 2016. Improved Representation Learning for Question Answer Matching. In *Proceedings of the 54th Annual Meeting of the Association for Computational Linguistics (Volume 1: Long Papers)*, pages 464–473, Berlin, Germany. Association for Computational Linguistics.

Kristian Woodsend and Mirella Lapata. 2014. Text Rewriting Improves Semantic Role Labeling. *Journal of Artificial Intelligence Research*, 51:133–164.

Fabio Massimo Zanzotto and Marco Pennacchiotti. 2010. Expanding textual entailment corpora from Wikipedia using co-training. In *Proceedings of the 2nd Workshop on The People's Web Meets NLP: Collaboratively Constructed Semantic Resources*, pages 28–36, Beijing, China. Coling 2010 Organizing Committee.

Sentiment Analysis and Lexical Cohesion for the Story Cloze Task

Michael Flor
Educational Testing Service
660 Rosedale Road
Princeton, NJ 08540
mflor@ets.org

Swapna Somasundaran
Educational Testing Service
660 Rosedale Road
Princeton, NJ 08540
ssomasundaran@ets.org

Abstract

We present two NLP components for the Story Cloze Task – dictionary-based sentiment analysis and lexical cohesion. While previous research found no contribution from sentiment analysis to the accuracy on this task, we demonstrate that sentiment is an important aspect. We describe a new approach, using a rule that estimates sentiment congruence in a story. Our sentiment-based system achieves strong results on this task. Our lexical cohesion system achieves accuracy comparable to previously published baseline results. A combination of the two systems achieves better accuracy than published baselines. We argue that sentiment analysis should be considered an integral part of narrative comprehension.

1 Introduction

The Story Cloze Task (SCT) is a novel challenge task in which an automated NLP system has to choose a correct ending for a short story, from two predefined alternatives. This new challenge stems from a long line of research on the types of knowledge that are required for narrative comprehension (Winograd, 1972; Schank and Abelson, 1977). Specifically, it is related to a previous type of challenge, the Narrative Cloze Task (NCT) (Chambers and Jurafsky, 2008).

The SCT departs from the narrow focus of the NCT. It is informed by the interest in the temporal and causal relations that form the intricate fabric of narrative stories. Some previous research on analyzing and learning commonsense information have focused on blogs (Gordon and Swanson, 2009; Manshadi et al., 2008), which are challenging and difficult texts. Other studies have focused on analysis of short fables (Goyal et al., 2013; Elson and McKeown, 2010). Mostafazadeh et al. (2016) produced a large curated corpus of simple commonsense stories, generated via crowdsourcing. Each story consists of exactly five short sentences, with a clear beginning, middle and ending, without embellishments, lengthy introductions and digressions.

For the Story Cloze Task, human authors used four-sentence core stories form the corpus, and provided two different ending sentences - a 'right' one and a 'wrong' one. Some of the 'wrong' endings include logical contradictions, some include events that are impossible or highly unlikely given our standard world knowledge. For example: 1. *Yesterday Stacey was driving to work.* 2. *Unfortunately a large SUV slammed into her.* 3. *Luckily she was alright.* 4. *However her car was destroyed.* Options: 5a. *Stacey got back in her car and drove to work* [wrong]. 5b. *Stacey told the police what happened* [right].

The current SCT has a validation set and a test set, with 1871 stories per set. Each story consists of four sentences, and two competing sentences as story endings. An NLP system is tasked to choose the correct ending from the two alternatives. Systems are evaluated on a simple accuracy measure (number of correct choices divided by number of stories). In this setting, if ending-choices are made randomly, the baseline success rate would be 50%.

In this paper we present our system for the SCT challenge. Section 2 outlines the approach, section 3 describes the algorithms and the results.

2 Approach

Our system is not designed for deep understanding of narrative or for semantic reasoning. The goal of our approach is to investigate the contribution of sentiment and affect in the SCT task. We

Proceedings of the 2nd Workshop on Linking Models of Lexical, Sentential and Discourse-level Semantics, pages 62–67,
Valencia, Spain, April 3, 2017. ©2017 Association for Computational Linguistics

build our system with components that perform sentiment analysis and estimate discourse cohesion. Our system tries to pick the most coherent ending based on the sentiment expectations that the story builds in the minds of the reader. For sentiment we consider positive and negative emotions, feelings, evaluations of the characters, as well as positive and negative situations and events (Wilson and Wiebe, 2005). In cases where sentiment is absent, we rely on lexical cohesion. Our approach is to investigate, if and how, coherence, as modeled using simple methods, can perform in the story completion task.

Consider this story with marked sentiment: 1. *Ron started his new job as a landscaper today* [neutral]. 2. *He loves the outdoors and has always enjoyed working in it* [positive]. 3. *His boss tells him to re-sod the front yard of the mayor's home* [neutral]. 4. *Ron is ecstatic, but does a thorough job and finishes super early* [positive]. Choices for ending (correct option is 5b): 5a. *Ron is immediately fired for insubordination* [negative]. 5b. *His boss commends him for a job well done* [positive].

In this story, there is a positive sequence of events. Hence it would be rather incoherent to have an ending that is starkly negative (incorrect option 5a). If indeed a negative ending were to be applied, it would be a twist in the story and would have to be indicated with a discourse marker to make the story coherent. In short stories, plot twists that relate to sentiment polarity are usually expressed via adverbial phrases, such as 'however', 'unfortunately' or 'luckily', and contrastive connectors, such as 'but' and 'yet'. Notably, some adverbials only indicate contrast to previous context (such as 'however'), while others induce a specific sentiment polarity. For example, 'luckily' indicates positive sentiment, overriding other sentiment-bearing words in the sentence; 'unfortunately' indicates negative sentiment, again overriding other indicators in the sentence. This is seen in the example below where a series of bad (negative) situations suddenly change for the better. The positive twist in the story is indicated by 'luckily'.

Example: 1. *Addie was working at the mall at Hollister when a strange man came in* [negative]. 2. *Before she knew it, Addie looked behind her and saw stolen clothes* [negative]. 3. *Addie got scared and tried to chase the man out* [negative]. 4. *Luckily guards came and arrested him* [overall positive, with an indication for positive story twist]. Ending options (correct is 5b): 5a. *Addie was put in jail for her crime* [negative]. 5b. *Addie was relieved and took deep breaths to calm herself* [positive].

In the absence of sentiment in a story, discourse coherence is, to some extent, captured by lexical cohesion. Take for example the following: 1. *Sam bought a new television. 2. It would not turn on. 3. He pressed the on button several times. 4. Finally Jeb came over to check it out.* Ending options (5b is correct): 5a. *Jeb turned on the microwave.* 5b. *Jeb plugged the television in and it turned on.* Here, even though both sentences introduce a new term ('microwave' and 'plugged'), the latter is semantically closer to the main story.

3   System Description

We construct two systems, one based on sentiment and another based on cohesion. We use the prediction from the sentiment-based system when the story has positive or negative sentiment elements, and back-off to a cohesion-based system when no sentiment is detected.

3.1   Sentiment-based system

Mostafazadeh et al. (2016) presented initial efforts to use sentiment analysis for the SCT. They used two approaches. Sentiment-Full: choose the ending that matches the average sentiment of the context (sentences 1-4). Sentiment-Last: choose the ending that matches the sentiment of the last context sentence. In both cases, they used the sentiment analysis component from the Stanford CoreNLP toolkit (Manning et al., 2014). No details were given on the algorithm they used for the story completion task. These respective models achieved accuracy of 0.489 and 0.514 on the validation set, and 0.492 and 0.522 on the test set.

For our analyses, we used an adapted version of the VADER sentiment dictionary. The original VADER dictionary (Hutto and Gilbert, 2014) contains 7062 lexical entries, with valence (sentiment) scores on the scale from -5 (very negative) to 5 (very positive). We expanded those lexical entries, and added all their inflectional variants, using an in-house English morphological toolkit. Our modified sentiment dictionary has 8255 entries. New words inherited the valence scores of origin words. For all entries, valence scores were rescaled into the range between -1 and 1.

For computing sentiment value for a sentence we filter out stop words (using a list of 250 common English stopwords) and analyze only content words. For each word, we retrieve its valence from the sentiment dictionary (if present), and sum up the values for the whole sentence. We implement local negation handling - if a sentiment-bearing word is negated (by a preceding word), the sentiment value of the word flips (multiply by -1) (Taboada et al., 2011). In addition we handle twists by checking for adverbials. If a sentence starts with a polarity-inducing adverbial, the sum of polarity values for the story is changed to the sign of the inducing adverbial (positive or negative). For this purpose, we prepared our own dictionary of polarity-inducing adverbials.

The key component in using sentiment scores for SCT is the decision rule: choose the completion sentence whose sentiment score is congruent with the rest of the story. The rule has two parts: a) Choose the completion sentence that has the same sentiment polarity as the preceding story. If the preceding story has positive (negative) sentiment, choose the positive (negative) completion. b) If both completions have same polarity, sign-congruence will not work. In such cases, we choose the completion whose value (magnitude) is closer to the sentiment value of the preceding context.

While analyzing the stories from the validation set with the VADER dictionary, we noted that 78% of the stories have sentiment-bearing words, both in the core sentences (sentences 1-4) and in at least one of the alternative ending sentences. The test set has an even higher percentage of such stories: 86%. The sentiment-based decision rule in the SCT cannot be applied in cases where the core-story or both completion sentences do not have a sentiment value. Thus, in order to test the effectiveness of our sentiment-based approach, we first tested its performance on sentiment-bearing stories only. Results are presented in Table 1. Note that the number of stories-with-sentiment depends on the lexicon. The results clearly indicate that considering the sentiment of the whole preceding context has a strong contribution towards selecting the correct ending (above 60% accuracy). Making a choice while considering the sentiment of only the last context sentence is much less successful (performance is worse than random).

We conducted a similar analysis with another lexicon – MPQA (Wilson et al., 2005), which has only binary valence values. It provided similar (al-

Set	Sentiment-Full	Sentiment-Last
Validation (1469)	0.679	0.436
Test (1610)	0.607	0.358

Table 1: Sytem accuracy on stories where sentiment is detected (in paretheses: number of stories with sentiment).

beit lower) results: 66% of stories in the validation set have sentiment, and accuracy on this set is 0.555. This indicates that even very simplified sentiment analysis has some utility for the SCT.

3.2 Lexical Cohesion

Our language model for lexical cohesion uses direct word-to-word associations (first-order word co-occurrences). This type of model has been successfully used for analyzing the contribution of lexical cohesion to readability and text difficulty of short reading materials (Flor and Beigman Klebanov, 2014). The current model was trained on the English Gigaword Fourth Edition corpus (Parker et al., 2009), approximately 2.5 billion word tokens. The model stores counts of word co-occurrence collected within paragraphs (rather than windows of set length). We use Positive Normalized PMI as our association measure. Normalized PMI was introduced by (Bouma, 2009); positive NPMI maps all negative values to zero. To calculate lexical cohesion between two sentences (or any other snippets of text), we use the following procedure. First, for each sentence we remove the stopwords. Then, we generate all pairs of words (so that one word comes from first sentence and the other word comes from the second sentence), retrieve their association values from the model, and sum up the values. The sum of pairwise associations can be used as a similarity (or relatedness) measure. We also experimented with average (dividing the sum by the number of pairs), but the sum performed slightly better in our experiments. For the SCT task, for each story, we computed lexical cohesion between sentences 1-4, taken together as a paragraph, and each of the competing completion sentences (LexCohesion Full). The decision rule is to choose the completion sentence that is more strongly associated with the preceding story. Accuracy is 0.534 on the validation set and 0.527 on the test set (with 1871 stories in each set). We also computed lexical cohesion between the last sentence of context and each of the competing endings (LexCohesion

Last). For this condition, accuracy is 0.556 on the validation set and 0.536 on the test set. Our results are comparable to those of (Mostafazadeh et al., 2016), who used vector-space embeddings and obtained 0.545 and 0.536 on the validation set, 0.539 and 0.522 on the test set.

3.3 Combining the Models

To provide a full algorithm for the SCT task, we use our sentiment-based algorithm, and only back off to our lexical cohesion model when sentiment is not detected in the story (sentences 1-4) or in neither of the ending sentences. Results are presented in Table 2. Best accuracy is achieved by combining the Sentiment-Full model with LexCohesion-Last: 0.654 on the validation set and 0.620 on the test set. These results outperform the previously published best baseline of 0.604 and 0.585 (Mostafazadeh et al., 2016).

Set	Sentiment-Full + LexCohesion-Full	Sentiment-Full + LexCohesion-Last
Validation	0.639	0.654
Test	0.618	0.620

Table 2: System accuracy on all stories in each set.

4 Discussion

The role of affect and emotion has long been noted for human story comprehension (Kneepkens and Zwaan, 1994; Miall, 1989) and in AI research on narratives (Lehnert and Vine, 1987; Dyer, 1983). Stories are typically about characters facing conflict. Sometimes the plot complications (negative events or situations) have to be overcome. In many such cases, one expects to encounter sentiment expressions in the story. Not surprisingly, we found that a large proportion of the stories, in both validation and test sets, have sentiment-bearing words. Thus, it is only natural to expect that sentiment analysis should be able to impact SCT. Our approach is to look at the polarity of sentiments and for sentiment congruence in a story. Using a sentiment dictionary that assigns sentiment values on a continuous scale, and looking only at lexically indicated sentiment, our algorithm chooses the correct ending in more than 60% of stories (when sentiment is detected).

We have demonstrated that even a rather simple, lexically-based sentiment analysis, can provide a considerable contribution to accuracy in the SCT. Our system only evaluates the congruence of two competing solutions, without attempting to develop a deep understanding of the story. For example, our system does not have the capability to reason that a car that has just been wrecked cannot be used to drive away. However, we consider that analyzing the sentiment of a story is not a shallow task (even if it is technically rather simple). We believe that human-level understanding of narrative involves many facets, including chains and schemas of events, plot units, character goals and states, etc. Handling each of them presents unique challenges to an NLP system. We argue that the sentiment aspect of narratives is one of the key aspects of stories. In fact, sentiment is a very deep aspect of narrative (Mar et al., 2011), one that we have only begun to explore. As the SCT focuses on very short stories, it is interesting to note that patterning of sentiment and affect has also been shown to exist on the scale of long novels (Reagan et al., 2016).

While our dictionary-based sentiment analysis was quite successful, we note that it should be viewed only as a starting point for investigating the role of sentiment in narrative comprehension. In the SCT, there are cases were dictionary-based sentiment detection fails to detect the sentiment in a story. For example: 1. *Brad went to the beach.* 2. *He made a sand castle.* 3. *He jumped into the ocean waters.* 4. *He swam with the small fish.* Options: 5a: *Brad's day went very badly.* 5b: *Brad then went home after a nice day.*

The above story has quite positive connotations, but none of the lexical terms from sentences 1-4 carry sentiment values in the dictionary. Our system detects sentiment in each of the competing ending sentences, but since no sentiment was detected in sentences 1-4, choice of the ending is relegated to lexical cohesion, rather than sentiment. A human reader would choose the second ending, based on positive sentiment connoted by the events.

5 Conclusion

In this paper we described a simple approach that combines sentiment- and cohesion-based systems for the Story Cloze Task. While previous research found sentiment analysis to be ineffective on this task, we proposed a new approach, using a rule that estimates sentiment congruence in a story. Our system achieves accuracy of 0.654 on the validation set and 0.620 on test set, mostly due to the strong contribution from sentiment analysis. Our results provide support to the notion that sentiment is an important aspect of narrative comprehension, and that sentiment-analysis can be a strong contributing factor for NLP analysis of stories. There are a number of avenues for further exploration, such as using machine learning methods to combine different types of information that go into making a story, using vector spaces, automated reasoning and extending the feature set to capture other aspects of language understanding.

References

Gerloff Bouma. 2009. Normalized (pointwise) mutual information in collocation extraction. In *From Form to Meaning: Processing Texts Automatically, Proceedings of the Biennial GSCL Conference*, pages 31–40. Gunter Narr Verlag, Tubingen.

Nathanael Chambers and Daniel Jurafsky. 2008. Unsupervised learning of narrative event chains. In *Proceedings of the 46th Annual Meeting of the ACL*, pages 789–797, Columbus, OH, USA, June. Association for Computational Linguistics, Association for Computational Linguistics.

Michael G. Dyer. 1983. The role of affect in narratives. *Cognitive Science*, 7:211–242.

David K. Elson and Kathleen R. McKeown. 2010. Building a bank of semantically encoded narratives. In Nicoletta Calzolari (Conference Chair), Khalid Choukri, Bente Maegaard, Joseph Mariani, Jan Odijk, Stelios Piperidis, Mike Rosner, and Daniel Tapias, editors, *Proceedings of the Seventh International Conference on Language Resources and Evaluation (LREC'10)*, Valletta, Malta. European Language Resources Association (ELRA).

Michael Flor and Beata Beigman Klebanov. 2014. Associative lexical cohesion as a factor in text complexity. *International Journal of Applied Linguistics*, 165(2):223–258.

Andrew S. Gordon and Reid Swanson. 2009. Identifying personal stories in millions of weblog entries. In *Third International Conference on Weblogs and Social Media, Data Challenge Workshop*, San Jose, CA, USA.

Amit Goyal, Ellen Riloff, and Hal Daume III. 2013. A computational model for plot units. *Computational Intelligence*, 3(29):466–488.

C.J. Hutto and Eric Gilbert. 2014. Vader: A parsimonious rule-based model for sentiment analysis of social media text. In *Proceedings of The 8th International AAAI Conference on Weblogs and Social Media (ICWSM14)*, Ann Arbor, MI, USA. Association for the Advancement of Artificial Intelligence.

E.W.E.M Kneepkens and Rolf A. Zwaan. 1994. Emotions and literary text comprehension. *Poetics*, 23:125–138.

Wendy G. Lehnert and Elaine W. Vine. 1987. The role of affect in narrative structure. *Cognition and Emotion*, 1(3):299–322.

Christopher Manning, Mihai Surdeanu, John Bauer, Jenny Finkel, Steven J. Bethard, and David McClosky. 2014. The stanford corenlp natural language processing toolkit. In *Proceedings of 52nd Annual Meeting of the Association for Computational Linguistics: System Demonstrations*, pages 55–60. Association for Computational Linguistics.

Mehdi Manshadi, Reid Swanson, and Andrew S. Gordon. 2008. Learning a probabilistic model of event sequences from internet weblog stories. In *Proceedings of 21st Conference of the Florida AI Society, Applied Natural Language Processing Track*, Coconut Grove, FL, USA.

Raymond A. Mar, Keith Oatley, Maja Djikic, and Justin Mullin. 2011. Emotion and narrative fiction: Interactive influences before, during, and after reading. *Cognition and Emotion*, 25(2):818–833.

David S. Miall. 1989. Affective comprehension of literary narratives. *Cognition and Emotion*, 3(1):55–78.

Nasrin Mostafazadeh, Nathanael Chambers, Xiaodong He, Devi Parikh, Dhruv Batra, Pushmeet Kohli Lucy Vanderwende, and James Allen. 2016. A corpus and cloze evaluation for deeper understanding of commonsense stories. In *Proceedings of the 2016 Conference of the North American Chapter of the Association for Computational Linguistics: Human Language Technologies (NAACL HLT)*, pages 839–849, San Diego, California. Association for Computational Linguistics.

Robert Parker, David Graff, Junbo Kong, Ke Chen, and Kazuaki Maeda. 2009. English gigaword fourth edition. https://catalog.ldc.upenn.edu/LDC2009T13.

Andrew J. Reagan, Lewis Mitchell, Dilan Kiley, Christopher M Danforth, and Peter Sheridan Dodds. 2016. The emotional arcs of stories are dominated by six basic shapes. *EPJ Data Science*, 5(31).

Roger C. Schank and Robert P. Abelson. 1977. *Scripts, Plans, Goals and Understanding*. Lawrence Erlbaum, Hillsdale, NJ, USA.

Maite Taboada, Julian Brooke, Milan Tofiloski, Kimberly Voll, and Manfred Stede. 2011. Lexiconbasedmethods for sentiment analysis. *Computational Linguistics*, 2(37):267–307.

Theresa Wilson and Janyce Wiebe. 2005. Annotating attributions and private states. In *Proceedings of ACL Workshop on Frontiers in Corpus Annotation II: Pie in the Sky*, pages 53–60, Ann Arbor, MI, USA. Association for Computational Linguistics.

Theresa Wilson, Janyce Wiebe, and Paul Hoffmann. 2005. Recognizing contextual polarity in phrase-level sentiment analysis. In *Proceedings of the Human Language Technologies Conference/Conference on Empirical Methods in Natural Language Processing (HLT/EMNLP-2005)*, pages 347–354, Vancouver. Association for Computational Linguistics.

Terry Winograd. 1972. *Understanding Natural Language*. Academic Press, Inc., Orlando, FL, USA.

Resource-Lean Modeling of Coherence in Commonsense Stories

Niko Schenk and **Christian Chiarcos**
Applied Computational Linguistics Lab
Goethe University Frankfurt am Main, Germany
{n.schenk,chiarcos}@em.uni-frankfurt.de

Abstract

We present a resource-lean neural recognizer for modeling coherence in commonsense stories. Our lightweight system is inspired by successful attempts to modeling discourse relations and stands out due to its simplicity and easy optimization compared to prior approaches to narrative script learning. We evaluate our approach in the Story Cloze Test[1] demonstrating an absolute improvement in accuracy of 4.7% over state-of-the-art implementations.

1 Introduction

Semantic applications related to Natural Language Understanding have seen a recent surge of interest within the NLP community, and *story understanding* can be regarded as one of the supreme disciplines in that field. Closely related to Machine Reading (Hovy, 2006) and script learning (Schank and Abelson, 1977; Mooney and DeJong, 1985), it is a highly challenging task which is built on top of a cascade of core NLP applications, including— among others—causal/temporal relation recognition (Mirza and Tonelli, 2016), event extraction (UzZaman and Allen, 2010), (implicit) semantic role labeling (Gerber and Chai, 2012; Schenk and Chiarcos, 2016) or inter-sentential discourse parsing (Mihaylov and Frank, 2016).

Recent progress has been made in the field of *narrative understanding*: a variety of successful approaches have been introduced, ranging from narrative chains (Chambers and Jurafsky, 2008) to script learning techniques (Regneri et al., 2010), or event schemas (Nguyen et al., 2015). What all these approaches have in common is that they ultimately seek to find a way to prototypically model the causal and correlational relationships between events, and also to obtain a structured (ideally more compact and abstract) representation of the underlying commonsense knowledge which is encoded in the respective story. The downside of these approaches is that they are feature-rich (potentially hand-crafted) and therefore costly and domain-specific to a large extent. On a related note, Mostafazadeh et al. (2016a) demonstrate that there is still room for improvement when testing the performances of these state-of-the-art techniques for learning procedural knowledge on an independent evaluation set.

Our Contribution: In this paper, we propose a lightweight, resource-lean framework for modeling procedural knowledge in commonsense stories whose only source of information are distributed word representations. We cast the problem of modeling text coherence as a special case of discourse processing in which our model jointly learns to distinguish correct from incorrect story endings. Our approach is inspired by promising related attempts using event embeddings and neural methods for script learning (Modi and Titov, 2014; Pichotta and Mooney, 2016). Our system is an end-to-end implementation of the ideas sketched in Mostafazadeh et al. (2016b) of the *joint paragraph and sentence level* model (cf. Section 3 for details). We evaluate our approach in the Story Cloze Test, a task for predicting story continuations. Despite its simplicity, our system demonstrates superior performance on the designated data over previous approaches to script learning and—due to its language and genre-independence—it also represents a solid basis for further optimization towards other textual domains.

---

[1]The shared task of the LSDSem 2017 workshop on *Linking Models of Lexical, Sentential and Discourse-level Semantics:*
http://www.coli.uni-saarland.de/~mroth/LSDSem/,
http://cs.rochester.edu/nlp/rocstories/LSDSem17/,
https://competitions.codalab.org/competitions/15333

Proceedings of the 2nd Workshop on Linking Models of Lexical, Sentential and Discourse-level Semantics, pages 68–73,
Valencia, Spain, April 3, 2017. ©2017 Association for Computational Linguistics

Four-Sentence Core Story	Quiz 1	Quiz 2
I asked Sarah out on a date. She said yes. I was so excited for our date together. We went to dinner and then a movie.	I had a terrible time. (*wrong* ending)	I got to kiss Sarah goodnight. (*correct* ending)

Table 1: An example of a *ROCStory* consisting of a core story and two alternative continuations.

2 The Story Cloze Test

2.1 Task Description

In the *Story Cloze Test* a participating system is presented with a four-sentence *core story* along with two alternative single-sentence endings, i.e. a correct and a wrong one. The system is then supposed to select the correct ending based on a semantic analysis of the individual story components. For this binary choice, outputs are evaluated on accuracy level.

2.2 Data

The shared task organizers provide participants with a large corpus of approx. 98k five-sentence everyday life stories (Mostafazadeh et al., 2016a, *ROCStories*[2]) for training their narrative story understanding models. Also a validation and a test set are available (each containing 1,872 instances). The former serves for parameter optimization, whereas final performance is evaluated on the test set. The instances in all three sets are mutually exclusive. Note that in addition to the *ROCStories*, both validation and test sets include an additional *wrong* 5th-sentence story ending (either in first or second position) plus hand-annotated decisions about which story ending is the right one. As an illustration, consider the example in Table 1 consisting of a core story and two alternative continuations (quizzes). The global semantics of this *ROCStory* is driven by two factors: i) a latent discoursive, temporal/causal relationship between the individual events in each sentence and ii) a resulting positive outcome of the story. Clearly, the right ending is the second quiz. Note that for all stories in the data set, the task of choosing the correct ending is human solvable with perfect agreement (Mostafazadeh et al., 2016a).

3 Approach

Our proposed model architecture for finding the right story continuation is inspired by novel works from (shallow) discourse parsing, most notably by the recent success of neural network-based frameworks in that field (Xue et al., 2016; Schenk et al., 2016; Wang and Lan, 2016). Specifically for *implicit* discourse relations, i.e. for those sentence pairs which, for instance, can signal a temporal, contrast or contingency relation, but which suffer from the absence of an explicit discourse marker (such as *but* or *because*), it has been shown that the interaction of properly tuned distributed representations over adjacent text spans can be particularly powerful in the relation classification task. We cast the Story Cloze test as a special case of implicit discourse relation recognition and attempt to model an underlying, latent connection between a core story and its correct vs. incorrect continuation. For instance, the final example sentence in the core story in Table 1 and the two adjacent quizzes could be treated as argument pairs (*Arg1* and *Arg2*) in the classical view of the Penn Discourse Treebank (Prasad et al., 2008), distinguishing different types of implicit discourse relations that hold between them.[3]

> *Arg1*: We went to dinner and then a movie.
> *Arg2*: I had a terrible time.
> TEMP.**SYNCHRONOUS**
>
> *Arg1*: We went to dinner and then a movie.
> *Arg2*: I got to kiss Sarah goodnight.
> TEMP.**ASYNCHRONOUS**.PRECEDENCE

Here, in the first example, the label SYN-CHRONOUS indicates that the two situations in both arguments overlap temporally (which could be signaled explicitly by *while*, for instance), whereas in the second example ASYN-CHRONOUS.PRECEDENCE implies a temporal or-

---

[2] http://cs.rochester.edu/nlp/rocstories/

[3] For details, see https://www.seas.upenn.edu/~pdtb/PDTBAPI/pdtb-annotation-manual.pdf

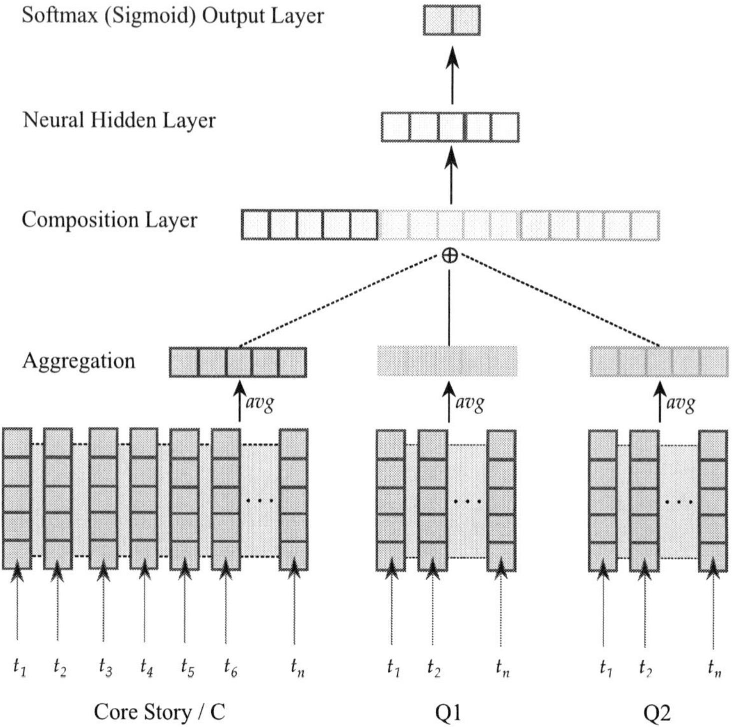

Figure 1: The proposed architecture for the Story Cloze Test. Depicted is a training instance consisting of three distributed word representation matrices for core story (C), quiz 1 (Q1) and quiz 2 (Q2), each component of varying length n. Note that either Q1 or Q2 is a wrong story ending. Matrices are first individually aggregated by average computation. Resulting vectors are then concatenated to form a composition unit which serves as input to the network with one hidden layer and binary output classification.

der of both events. The distinction between different implicit discourse senses are subtle nuances and are highly challenging to detect automatically; however, they are typical of the *ROCStories*, as almost no explicit discourse markers are present between the individual story sentences. Finally, note that our motivation for this approach is also related to the classical view of recognizing *textual entailment* which would treat correct and wrong endings as the entailing and contradicting hypotheses, respectively (Giampiccolo et al., 2007; Mostafazadeh et al., 2016a).

3.1 Training Instances

For the Story Cloze Test, we model a training instance as a triplet consisting of the four-sentence core story (C), a first quiz sentence (Q1) *and* a second quiz sentence (Q2) from which either Q1 or Q2 is the correct continuation of the story. Note that the original *ROCStories* contain only valid five-sentence sequences but the evaluation data requires a system to select from a pool of two alternatives. Therefore, for each single story in *ROCStories*, we randomly sample one negative (wrong) continuation Q_{wrong} from all last sentences, and generate two training instances with the following patterns:

[C, Q1, Q2$_{wrong}$]:Label_1,[C, Q1$_{wrong}$, Q2]:Label_2, where the label indicates the position of the correct quiz. Our motivation is to jointly learn core stories together with their true ending while at the same time discriminating them from semantically irrelevant continuations.

For each component in the triplet, we have experimented with a variety of different calculations in order to capture their idiosyncratic syntactic and semantic properties. We found the vector average over their respective words $\vec{v}^{avg} = \frac{1}{N} \sum_{i=1}^{N} E(t_i)$ to perform reasonably well, where N is the total number of tokens filling either of C, Q1 or Q2, respectively, resulting in three individual vector representations. Here, we define $E(\cdot)$ as an embedding function which maps a token t_i to its distributed representation, i.e., a precomputed vector of d dimensions. As distributed word representations, we chose out of the box vectors; GloVe vectors (Pennington et al., 2014), dependency-based word embeddings (Levy and Goldberg, 2014) and the pre-trained Google News vectors with $d = 300$ from *word2vec*[4] (Mikolov et al., 2013). Using the same tool, we also trained custom embeddings (bag-of-words and skip-gram) with 300 dimensions on the *ROCStories* corpus.[5]

3.2 Network Architecture

The feature construction process and the neural network architecture are depicted in Figure 1. The bottom part illustrates how tokens are mapped through three stacked embedding matrices for C, Q1 and Q2, each of dimensionality $\mathbb{R}^{d \times n}$. A second step applies the average aggregation and concatenates the so-obtained vectors $\vec{c}^{avg}, \vec{q_1}^{avg}, \vec{q_2}^{avg}$ (each $\vec{v}^{avg} \in \mathbb{R}^d$) into an overall composed story representation of dimensionality $\mathbb{R}^{3*d}$ which in turn serves as input to a feedforward neural network. The network is set up with one hidden layer and one sigmoid output layer for binary label classification for the position of the correct ending, i.e. first or second.

3.3 Implementational Details

The network is trained only on the *ROCStories* (and the negative training items), totaling approx. 200k training instances, over 30 iterations and 35 epochs with pretraining and a mini batch size of 120. All (hyper-)parameters are chosen and optimized on the validation set. We conduct data normalization, Xavier weight initialization (Glorot and Bengio, 2010) on the input layer, and employ rectified linear unit activation functions to both the composition layer and hidden layer with 220-250 nodes, and finally apply a sigmoid output layer for label classification. The learning rate is set to 0.04, l2 regularization = 0.0002 for penalizing network weights using the cross entropy error loss function. The network is trained using stochastic gradient descent and backpropagation implemented in the toolkit *deeplearning4j*.[6]

System	Performance	
	Validation	Test
DSSM	0.604	0.585
Narrative-Chains	0.510	0.494
Majority Class	0.514	0.513
Neural-ROCStoriesOnly	**0.629**	0.632
SVM-ManualLabels	–	**0.700**

Table 2: Performances (in % accuracy) on the validation and test sets of The Story Cloze Test.

4 Evaluation

We evaluate our model intrinsically on both validation and test set provided by the shared task organizers. As a reference, we also provide three baselines borrowed from Mostafazadeh et al. (2016a) at the time when the data set was released, namely the best-performing algorithms inspired by Huang et al. (2013, Deep Structured Semantic Model/DSSM) and Chambers and Jurafsky (2008, Narrative-Chains). Table 2 shows that correct endings appear almost equally often in either first or second position in the annotated data sets. The majority class is only significantly beaten by the DSSM model. Our approach (denoted by *Neural-ROCStoriesOnly*), however, can further improve upon the best system by an absolute increase in accuracy of 4.7%. Only the best configuration is shown and has been achieved with the 300-dimensional pre-trained Google News embeddings. Interestingly, the performance of the model on the test set is slightly better that on the validation set but also very similar which suggests that it is able to generalize well to unseen data and is not prone to overfitting training or validation data. A manual inspection of a subset of the misclassified items reveals that our neural recognizer is struggling to properly handle story continuations which change the underlying sentiment of the core story either towards negative or positive, e.g. *fail test, study hard → pass test*. In future work we plan to address this issue in closer detail.

A Note on the Evaluation & Training Procedure: Although the task has been stated differently, it stands to reason that one could exploit the tiny amount of hand-annotated data in the validation set directly to train a classifier. We have done so as a side experiment using as features the

---

[4]`https://code.google.com/p/word2vec/`
[5]We remove punctuation symbols in all settings.
[6]`https://deeplearning4j.org/`

same 900-dimensional composition layer embeddings from Section 3.2 and optimized a minimalist SVM classifier by 10-fold cross-validation, with feature and parameter selection on the validation set.[7] The final model achieves a test set accuracy of 70.02%, cf. *SVM-ManualLabels* in Table 2. Besides the relatively good performance obtained here, however, we want to emphasize that— when no hand-annotated labels for the correct position of the quizzes are available—the *Neural-ROCStories* approach introduced in Section 3 represents a promising and more generic framework for coherence learning, incorporating the plain text *ROCStories* as only source of information.

5   Conclusion & Outlook

In this paper, we have introduced a highly generic and resource-lean neural recognizer for modeling text coherence, which has been adapted to a designated data set—the *ROCStories* for modeling story continuations. Our approach is inspired by successful models for (implicit) discourse relation classification and only relies on the carefully tuned interaction of distributed word representations between story components.

An evaluation shows that state-of-the-art algorithms for script learning can be outperformed by our model. Future work should address the incorporation of linguistic knowledge into the currently rather rigid representations of the story sentences, including sentiment polarities or weighted syntactic dependencies (Schenk et al., 2016). Even though it has been claimed that the simpler feedforward neural networks do perform better in the discourse modeling task (Rutherford and Xue, 2016), it remains an open and challenging topic for future experiments on the *ROCStories*, whether *recurrent* architectures (Pichotta and Mooney, 2016) can have additional value towards a deeper story understanding.[8]

Acknowledgments

We want to thank Philip Schulz for constructive feedback regarding the neural network setup and the two anonymous reviewers for their very helpful remarks and insightful comments.

---

[7]We used *libsvm* (https://www.csie.ntu.edu.tw/~cjlin/libsvm/), RBF kernel, $c = 1.85$, $g = 0.63$.

[8]The code for this study is publicly available from the following URL: http://www.acoli.informatik.uni-frankfurt.de/resources/.

References

Nathanael Chambers and Daniel Jurafsky. 2008. Unsupervised Learning of Narrative Event Chains. In *ACL 2008, Proceedings of the 46th Annual Meeting of the Association for Computational Linguistics, June 15-20, 2008, Columbus, Ohio, USA*, pages 789–797.

Matthew Gerber and Joyce Chai. 2012. Semantic Role Labeling of Implicit Arguments for Nominal Predicates. *Comput. Linguist.*, 38(4):755–798, December.

Danilo Giampiccolo, Bernardo Magnini, Ido Dagan, and Bill Dolan. 2007. The Third PASCAL Recognizing Textual Entailment Challenge. In *Proceedings of the ACL-PASCAL Workshop on Textual Entailment and Paraphrasing*, RTE '07, pages 1–9, Stroudsburg, PA, USA. Association for Computational Linguistics.

Xavier Glorot and Yoshua Bengio. 2010. Understanding the difficulty of training deep feedforward neural networks. In *In Proceedings of the International Conference on Artificial Intelligence and Statistics (AISTATS10). Society for Artificial Intelligence and Statistics*.

Eduard H. Hovy. 2006. Learning by Reading: An Experiment in Text Analysis. In Petr Sojka, Ivan Kopecek, and Karel Pala, editors, *TSD*, volume 4188 of *Lecture Notes in Computer Science*, pages 3–12. Springer.

Po-Sen Huang, Xiaodong He, Jianfeng Gao, Li Deng, Alex Acero, and Larry Heck. 2013. Learning Deep Structured Semantic Models for Web Search Using Clickthrough Data. In *Proceedings of the 22Nd ACM International Conference on Information & Knowledge Management*, CIKM '13, pages 2333–2338, New York, NY, USA. ACM.

Omer Levy and Yoav Goldberg. 2014. Dependency-Based Word Embeddings. In *Proceedings of the 52nd Annual Meeting of the Association for Computational Linguistics, ACL 2014, June 22-27, 2014, Baltimore, MD, USA, Volume 2: Short Papers*, pages 302–308.

Todor Mihaylov and Anette Frank. 2016. Discourse Relation Sense Classification Using Cross-argument Semantic Similarity Based on Word Embeddings. In *Proceedings of the CoNLL-16 shared task*, pages 100–107. Association for Computational Linguistics.

Tomas Mikolov, Kai Chen, Greg Corrado, and Jeffrey Dean. 2013. Efficient Estimation of Word Representations in Vector Space. In *Proceedings of Workshop at International Conference on Learning Representations*.

Paramita Mirza and Sara Tonelli. 2016. CATENA: causal and temporal relation extraction from natural language texts. In *COLING 2016, 26th International Conference on Computational Linguistics,*

Proceedings of the Conference: Technical Papers, December 11-16, 2016, Osaka, Japan, pages 64–75.

Ashutosh Modi and Ivan Titov. 2014. Learning Semantic Script Knowledge with Event Embeddings. In *Proceedings of the 2nd International Conference on Learning Representations (Workshop track)*, Banff, Canada.

Raymond J. Mooney and Gerald DeJong. 1985. Learning Schemata for Natural Language Processing. In *Proceedings of the 9th International Joint Conference on Artificial Intelligence. Los Angeles, CA, USA, August 1985*, pages 681–687.

Nasrin Mostafazadeh, Nathanael Chambers, Xiaodong He, Devi Parikh, Dhruv Batra, Lucy Vanderwende, Pushmeet Kohli, and James Allen. 2016a. A Corpus and Cloze Evaluation for Deeper Understanding of Commonsense Stories. In *Proceedings of the 2016 Conference of the North American Chapter of the Association for Computational Linguistics: Human Language Technologies*, pages 839–849, San Diego, California, June. Association for Computational Linguistics.

Nasrin Mostafazadeh, Lucy Vanderwende, Wen-tau Yih, Pushmeet Kohli, and James Allen. 2016b. Story Cloze Evaluator: Vector Space Representation Evaluation by Predicting What Happens Next. In *Proceedings of the 1st Workshop on Evaluating Vector-Space Representations for NLP*, pages 24–29, Berlin, Germany, August. Association for Computational Linguistics.

Kiem-Hieu Nguyen, Xavier Tannier, Olivier Ferret, and Romaric Besançon. 2015. Generative Event Schema Induction with Entity Disambiguation. In *Proceedings of the 53rd Annual Meeting of the Association for Computational Linguistics and the 7th International Joint Conference on Natural Language Processing of the Asian Federation of Natural Language Processing, ACL 2015, July 26-31, 2015, Beijing, China, Volume 1: Long Papers*, pages 188–197.

Jeffrey Pennington, Richard Socher, and Christopher D. Manning. 2014. Glove: Global vectors for word representation. In *Empirical Methods in Natural Language Processing (EMNLP)*, pages 1532–1543.

Karl Pichotta and Raymond J. Mooney. 2016. Using sentence-level LSTM language models for script inference. In *Proceedings of the 54th Annual Meeting of the Association for Computational Linguistics, ACL 2016, August 7-12, 2016, Berlin, Germany, Volume 1: Long Papers*.

Rashmi Prasad, Nikhil Dinesh, Alan Lee, Eleni Miltsakaki, Livio Robaldo, Aravind Joshi, and Bonnie Webber. 2008. The Penn Discourse TreeBank 2.0. In *Proceedings, 6th International Conference on Language Resources and Evaluation*, pages 2961–2968, Marrakech, Morocco.

Michaela Regneri, Alexander Koller, and Manfred Pinkal. 2010. Learning script knowledge from web experiments. In *Proceedings of the 48th Annual Meeting of the Association for Computational Linguistics (ACL)*, Uppsala.

Attapol Rutherford and Nianwen Xue. 2016. Robust Non-Explicit Neural Discourse Parser in English and Chinese. In *Proceedings of the CoNLL-16 shared task*, pages 55–59. Association for Computational Linguistics.

Roger C. Schank and Robert P. Abelson. 1977. *Scripts, Plans, Goals and Understanding: an Inquiry into Human Knowledge Structures*. L. Erlbaum, Hillsdale, NJ.

Niko Schenk and Christian Chiarcos. 2016. Unsupervised learning of prototypical fillers for implicit semantic role labeling. In *NAACL HLT 2016, The 2016 Conference of the North American Chapter of the Association for Computational Linguistics: Human Language Technologies, San Diego California, USA, June 12-17, 2016*, pages 1473–1479.

Niko Schenk, Christian Chiarcos, Kathrin Donandt, Samuel Rönnqvist, Evgeny Stepanov, and Giuseppe Riccardi. 2016. Do We Really Need All Those Rich Linguistic Features? A Neural Network-Based Approach to Implicit Sense Labeling. In *Proceedings of the CoNLL-16 shared task*, pages 41–49. Association for Computational Linguistics.

Naushad UzZaman and James F Allen. 2010. Extracting Events and Temporal Expressions from Text. In *Semantic Computing (ICSC), 2010 IEEE Fourth International Conference on*, pages 1–8. IEEE.

Jianxiang Wang and Man Lan. 2016. Two End-to-end Shallow Discourse Parsers for English and Chinese in CoNLL-2016 Shared Task. In *Proceedings of the CoNLL-16 shared task*, pages 33–40. Association for Computational Linguistics.

Nianwen Xue, Hwee Tou Ng, Sameer Pradhan, Bonnie Webber, Attapol Rutherford, Chuan Wang, and Hongmin Wang. 2016. The CoNLL-2016 Shared Task on Shallow Discourse Parsing. In *Proceedings of the Twentieth Conference on Computational Natural Language Learning - Shared Task*, Berlin, Germany, August. Association for Computational Linguistics.

An RNN-based Binary Classifier for the Story Cloze Test

Melissa Roemmele
Institute for Creative Technologies
University of Southern California
`roemmele@ict.usc.edu`

Sosuke Kobayashi[*]
Preferred Networks, Inc.
`sosk@preferred.jp`

Naoya Inoue
Tohoku University
`naoya-i@ecei.tohoku.ac.jp`

Andrew M. Gordon
Institute for Creative Technologies
University of Southern California
`gordon@ict.usc.edu`

Abstract

The Story Cloze Test consists of choosing a sentence that best completes a story given two choices. In this paper we present a system that performs this task using a supervised binary classifier on top of a recurrent neural network to predict the probability that a given story ending is correct. The classifier is trained to distinguish correct story endings given in the training data from incorrect ones that we artificially generate. Our experiments evaluate different methods for generating these negative examples, as well as different embedding-based representations of the stories. Our best result obtains 67.2% accuracy on the test set, outperforming the existing top baseline of 58.5%.

1 Introduction

Automatically predicting "what happens next" in a story is an emerging AI task, situated at the point where natural language processing meets commonsense reasoning research. Story understanding began as classic AI planning research (Meehan, 1977, e.g.), and has evolved with the shift to data-driven AI approaches by which large sets of stories can be analyzed from text (Granroth-Wilding and Clark, 2016; Li et al., 2013; McIntyre and Lapata, 2009, e.g.). A barrier to this research has been the lack of standard evaluation schemes for benchmarking progress. The new Story Cloze Test (Mostafazadeh et al., 2016) addresses this need through a binary-choice evaluation format: given the beginning sentences of a story, the task is to choose which of two given sentences best completes the story. The cloze framework also

provides training stories (referred to here as the ROC corpus) in the same domain as the evaluation items. Mostafazadeh et al. details the crowdsourced authoring process for this dataset. Ultimately the training data consists of 97,027 five-sentence stories. The separate cloze test has 3742 items (divided equally between validation and test sets) each containing the first four sentences of a story with a correct and incorrect ending to choose from.

In the current paper, we describe a set of approaches for performing the Story Cloze Test. Our best result obtains 67.2% accuracy on the test set, outperforming Mostafazadeh et al.'s best baseline of 58.5%. We first report two additional unsupervised baselines used in other narrative prediction tasks. We then describe our supervised approach, which uses a recurrent neural network (RNN) with a binary classifier to distinguish correct story endings from artificially generated incorrect endings. We compare the performance of this model when alternatively trained on different story encodings and different strategies for generating incorrect endings.

2 Story Representations

We examined two ways of representing stories in our models, both of which encode stories as vectors of real numbers known as embeddings. This was motivated by the top performing baseline in Mostafazadeh et al. which used embeddings to select the candidate story ending with the higher cosine similarity to its context.

Word Embeddings: We first tried encoding stories with word-level embeddings using the word2vec model (Mikolov et al., 2013), which learns to represent words as n-dimensional vector of real values based on neighboring words. We compared two different sets of vectors: 300-

---

[*]This research was conducted at his previous affiliation, Tohoku University.

Proceedings of the 2nd Workshop on Linking Models of Lexical, Sentential and Discourse-level Semantics, pages 74–80,
Valencia, Spain, April 3, 2017. ©2017 Association for Computational Linguistics

dimension vectors trained on the 100-billion word Google News dataset[1] and 300-dimension vectors that we trained on ROC corpus itself. The latter were trained using the gensim word2vec library[2], with a window size of 10 words and negative sampling of 25 noise words. All other parameters were set to the default values given by the library. By comparing these two sets of embeddings, we intended to determine the extent to which our models can rely only on the limited training data provided for this task. In our supervised experiments we averaged the embeddings of the words in each sentence, resulting in a single vector representation of the entire sentence.

Sentence Embeddings: The second embedding strategy we used was the skip-thought model (Kiros et al., 2015), which produces vectors that encode an entire sentence. Analogous to training word vectors by predicting nearby words, the skip-thought vectors are trained to predict nearby sentences. We evaluated two sets of sentence vectors: 4800-dimension vectors trained on the 11,000 books in the BookCorpus dataset[3], and 2400-dimension vectors we trained ourselves on the ROC corpus[4]. The latter BookCorpus vectors were also used in a baseline that measured vector similarity between the story context and candidate endings in Mostafazadeh et al.

3 Unsupervised Approaches

Mostafazadeh et al. applied several unsupervised baselines to the Story Cloze Test. We evaluated two additional approaches due to their success on other narrative prediction tasks.

Average Maximum Similarity (AveMax): The AveMax model is a slight variation on Mostafazadeh et al.'s averaged word2vec baseline. It is currently implemented to predict story continuations from user input in the recently developed DINE application[5]. Instead of selecting the embedded candidate ending most similar to the context, this method iterates through each word in the ending, finds the word in the context with most similar embedding, and then takes the mean of these maximum similarity embeddings. We evaluated this method using both the word embeddings

from the Google News dataset and the ROC corpus.

Pointwise Mututal Information (PMI): The PMI model was used successfully on the Choice of Plausible Alternatives task (COPA) (Roemmele et al., 2011; Gordon et al., 2011; Gordon et al., 2012; Luo et al., 2016) which similarly to the Story Cloze Test uses a binary-choice format to elicit inferences about a segment of narrative text. This model relies on lexical co-occurrence counts (of raw words rather than embeddings) to compute a 'causality score' about how likely one sentence is to follow another in a story. We applied the same approach to the Story Cloze Test to select the final sentence with the higher causality score of the two candidates. We evaluated word counts from two different sources: a corpus of one million stories extracted from personal weblogs (as was used in Gordon et al.) and the ROC corpus.

4 Supervised Approaches

Given the moderate size of the ROC corpus at almost 100,000 stories, and that the Story Cloze Test can be viewed as a classification task choosing from two possible outputs, we investigated a supervised approach. Unlike the training data for traditional classification models, the ROC corpus does not involve a set of discrete categories by which stories are labeled. Moreover, while the Story Cloze Test provides a correct and incorrect outcome to choose from, the training data only contains the correct ending for a given story. So our strategy was to create a new training set with binary labels of 1 for correct endings (positive examples) and 0 for incorrect endings (negative examples). Each story in the corpus was considered a positive example. Given a positive example, we generated a negative example by replacing its final sentence with an incorrect ending. As described below, we generated more than one negative ending per story, so that each positive example had multiple negative counterparts. Our methods for generating negative examples are described in the next section. Our approach was to train a binary classifier to distinguish between these positive and negative examples.

The binary classifier is integrated with an RNN. RNNs have been used successfully for other narrative modeling tasks (Iyyer et al., 2016; Pichotta and Mooney, 2016). Our model takes the context sentences and ending for a particular story as in-

---

[1]https://code.google.com/archive/p/word2vec/

[2]https://radimrehurek.com/gensim/models/word2vec.html

[3]https://github.com/ryankiros/skip-thoughts

[4]We used the same code and default parameters available at the above GitHub page.

[5]http://dine.ict.usc.edu

Context	Correct	Type	Incorrect
Hal was walking	Finally	**Rand**	Tom was kicked out of the game.
his dog one	Hal lured	**Back**	A cat ran across their path.
morning. A cat	him back	**Near**	His dog had to wear a leg cast for weeks.
ran across their	to his	**Near**	His dog is too fast and runs off.
path. Hal's dog	side.	**Near**	Rod realized he should have asked before petting the dog.
strained so hard,			
the leash broke!		**LM**	When she woke up, she realized he had no dog noises.
He chased the cat		**LM**	When he got to the front, he saw a dog, squirrel, and dog.
for several			
minutes.		**LM**	When he got to the front office, he found a cat in the ditch.
John woke up	John	**Rand**	She waited for months for her hair to grow back out.
sick today. He	dropped	**Back**	He put a bowl of soup into the microwave.
washed his face	the soup	**Near**	Dan returned to the couch and watched a movie with his snack.
in the bathroom.	when he		
John went into	grabbed	**Near**	The doctor gave him medicine to get better.
the kitchen to	it from the	**Near**	Finally, he ate it.
make some soup.	microwave.	**LM**	He brushed his teeth and ate it for a while, he was sad.
He put a bowl of		**LM**	He put the bowl in his microwave, and went to the kitchen.
soup into the			
microwave.		**LM**	He brushed her teeth, but the candles didn't feel so he didn't have any.

Table 1: Examples of generated negative endings

put and then returns the probability of that ending being correct, using the ending labels as feedback during training. Specifically, we combine the sentence representations of the context and final sentences into one sequence and feed each sentence as a timestep into a single 1000-node GRU (Cho et al., 2014) hidden layer. The values of the final hidden state are given to a top feed-forward layer composed of one node with sigmoid activation. A binary cross-entropy objective function is applied to train the network to maximize the probability of positive examples being correct. All experiments used RMSprop (Hinton et al., 2012) with a batch size of 100 to optimize the model over 10 training epochs. After training, given a cloze test item, the model predicted a probability score for each candidate ending, and the ending with the higher score was selected as the response for that item.

5 Incorrect Ending Generation

We examined four different ways to generate the incorrect endings for the classifier. Table 1 shows examples of each.

Random (Rand): First, we simply replaced each story's ending with a randomly selected ending from a different story in the training set. In most cases this ending will not be semantically related to the story context, so this approach would be expected to predict endings based strictly on semantic overlap with the context.

Backward (Back): The Random approach generates negative examples in which the semantics of the context and ending are most often far apart. However, these examples may not represent the items in the Story Cloze Test, where the endings generally both have some degree of semantic coherence with the context sentences. To generate negative examples in the same semantic space as the correct ending, we replaced the fifth sentence of a given story with one of its four context sentences (i.e. a backward sentence). This results in an ending that is semantically related to the story, but is typically incoherent given its repetition in the story.

Nearest-Ending (Near): The Nearest-Ending approach aims to find endings that are very close to the correct ending by using an ending for a similar story in the corpus. Swanson and Gordon (2012) presented this model in their interactive storytelling system. Given a story context, we retrieved the most similar story in the corpus (in terms of cosine similarity), and then projected the final sentence of the similar story as the ending of the given story. Multiple endings were produced by finding the N most similar stories. The negative examples generated by this scheme can be seen as 'almost' positive examples with likely coherence errors, given the sparsity of the corpus. This is in line with the cloze task where both endings are plausible, but the correct answer is more likely than the other.

Language Model (LM): Separate from the binary classifier, we trained an RNN-based language model (Mikolov et al., 2010) on the ROC corpus. The LM learns a conditional probability distribution indicating the chance of each possible word appearing in a sequence given the words that precede it. During training, the LM iterated through a story word by word, each time updating its predicted probability of the next observed word. During generation, we gave the LM the context of each training story and had it produce a final sentence by sampling words one by one according to the predicted distribution, as described in Sutskever et al. (2011). Multiple sentences were generated for the same story by sampling the N most probable words at each timestep. The LM had a 200-node embedding layer and two 500-node GRU layers, and was trained using the Adam optimizer (Kingma and Ba, 2015) with a batch size of 50. This approach has an advantage over the Nearest-Ending method in that it leverages all the stories in the training data for generation, rather than predicting an ending based on a single story. Thus, it can generate endings that are not directly observed in the training corpus. Like the nearest-ending approach, an ideal LM would be expected to generate positive examples similar to the original stories it is trained on. However, we found that the LM-generated endings were relevant to the story context but had less of a commonsense interpretation than the provided endings, again likely due to training data sparsity.

6 Experiments

We trained a classifier for each type of negative ending and additionally for each type of embedding, shown in Table 2. For each correct example, we generated multiple incorrect examples. We found that setting the number of negative samples per positive example near 6 pro-

duced the best results on the validation set for all configurations, so we kept this number consistent across experiments. The exception is the Backward method, which can only generate one of the first four sentences in each story. For each generation method, the negative samples were kept the same across runs of the model with different embeddings, rather than re-sampling for each run. After discovering that our best validation results came from the random endings, we also evaluated combinations of these endings with the other types to see if they could further boost the model's performance. The samples used by these combined-method experiments were a subset of the negative samples generated for the single-method results.

Table 2 shows the accuracy of all unsupervised and supervised models on both the validation and test sets, with the best test result within each group in bold. Among the unsupervised models, the AveMax model with the GoogleNews embeddings (55.2% test accuracy) performs comparably to Mostafazadeh et al.'s word2vec similarity model (53.9%). The PMI approach performs at the same level as the current best baseline of 58.5%, and the counts from the ROC stories are just as effective (59.9%) as those from the much larger blog corpus (59.1%).

The best test result using the GoogleNews word embeddings (61.5%) was slightly better than that of the ROC word embeddings (58.8%). Among the single-method results, the word embeddings were outperformed by the best result of the skip-thought embeddings (63.2%), suggesting that the skip-thought model may capture more information about a sentence than simply averaging its word embeddings. For this reason we skipped evaluating the word embeddings for the combined-ending experiments. One caveat to this is the smaller size of the word embeddings relative to the skip-thought vectors. While it is unusual for word2vec embeddings to have more than a thousand dimensions, to be certain that the difference in performance was not due to the difference in dimensionality, we performed an ad-hoc evaluation of word embeddings that were the same size as the ROC sentence vectors (2400 nodes). We computed these vectors from the ROC corpus in the same way described in Section 2, and applied them to our best-performing data configuration (Rand-3 + Back-1 + Near-1 + LM-1). The result (57.9%) was still lower than that produced by the cor-

	Val	Test
Unsupervised		
AveMax		
GoogleNews WordEmb	0.553	**0.552**
ROC WordEmb	0.548	0.547
PMI		
Blog Corpus	0.585	0.591
ROC Corpus	0.581	**0.599**
Supervised		
Rand-6		
GoogleNews WordEmb	0.625	0.585
ROC WordEmb	0.605	0.584
BookCorpus SentEmb	0.645	**0.632**
ROC SentEmb	0.639	0.631
Back-4		
GoogleNews WordEmb	0.529	0.540
ROC WordEmb	0.528	0.553
BookCorpus SentEmb	0.545	0.539
ROC SentEmb	0.548	**0.560**
Near-6		
GoogleNews WordEmb	0.641	0.615
ROC WordEmb	0.585	0.588
BookCorpus SentEmb	0.649	**0.621**
ROC SentEmb	0.632	0.615
LM-6		
GoogleNews WordEmb	0.524	0.534
ROC WordEmb	0.523	**0.544**
BookCorpus SentEmb	0.520	0.507
ROC SentEmb	0.514	0.512
Rand-4 + Back-2		
BookCorpus SentEmb	0.662	**0.669**
ROC SentEmb	0.664	0.664
Rand-4 + Near-2		
BookCorpus SentEmb	0.636	**0.641**
ROC SentEmb	0.650	0.609
Rand-4 + LM-2		
BookCorpus SentEmb	0.624	0.607
ROC SentEmb	0.640	**0.653**
Rand-3 + Back-1 + Near-1 + LM-1		
ROC WordEmb (2400)	0.599	0.579
BookCorpus SentEmb	0.656	**0.672**
ROC SentEmb	0.680	0.661

Table 2: Accuracy on the Story Cloze Test

responding ROC sentence embeddings (66.1%), supporting our idea that the skip-thought embeddings are a better sentence representation. Interestingly, though the BookCorpus sentence vectors obtained the best result overall (67.2%), they performed on average the same as the ROC ones (mean accuracy of 61.1% versus 61.3%, respectively), despite that the former have more dimensions (4800) and were trained on several more stories. This might suggest it helps to model the unique genre of stories contained in the ROC corpus for this task.

The best results in terms of data generation incorporate the Random endings, suggesting that for many of the items in the Story Cloze Test, the correct ending is the one that is more semantically similar to the context. Not surprisingly, the Backward endings have limited effect on their own (best result 56%), but they boost the performance of the Random endings when combined (best result 66.9%). We expected that the Nearest-Ending and LM endings would have an advantage over the Random endings, but our results didn't show this. The best result for the Nearest-Ending method was 62.1% compared to 63.2% produced by the Random endings. The LM endings fared particularly badly on their own (best result 54.4%). We noticed the LM seemed to produce very similar endings across different stories, which possibly influenced this result. The best result overall (67.2%) was produced by the model that sampled from all four types of endings, though it was only trivially higher than the best result for the combined Random and Backward endings (66.9%). Still, we see opportunity in the technique of using generative methods to expand the training set. We only generated incorrect endings in this work, but ideally this approach could generate correct endings as well, given that a story has multiple possible correct endings. It is possible that the small size of the ROC corpus limited our current success with this idea, so in the future we plan to pursue this using a much larger story dataset.

7   Acknowledgments

The projects or efforts depicted were or are sponsored by the U. S. Army. The content or information presented does not necessarily reflect the position or the policy of the Government, and no official endorsement should be inferred. Additionally, this work was partially supported by JSPS KAKENHI Grant Numbers 15H01702, 16H06614, and CREST, JST.

References

Kyunghyun Cho, Bart van Merrienboer, Dzmitry Bahdanau, and Yoshua Bengio. 2014. On the properties of neural machine translation: Encoder-decoder approaches. In *Proceedings of SSST-8, Eighth Workshop on Syntax, Semantics and Structure in Statistical Translation*, pages 103–111, Doha, Qatar, October. Association for Computational Linguistics.

Andrew S. Gordon, Cosmin Adrian Bejan, and Kenji Sagae. 2011. Commonsense causal reasoning using millions of personal stories. In *Proceedings of the Twenty-Fifth AAAI Conference on Artificial Intelligence*, AAAI'11, pages 1180–1185. AAAI Press.

Andrew S. Gordon, Zornitsa Kozareva, and Melissa Roemmele. 2012. Semeval-2012 task 7: Choice of plausible alternatives: An evaluation of commonsense causal reasoning. In *Proceedings of the First Joint Conference on Lexical and Computational Semantics - Volume 1: Proceedings of the Main Conference and the Shared Task, and Volume 2: Proceedings of the Sixth International Workshop on Semantic Evaluation*, SemEval '12, pages 394–398, Stroudsburg, PA, USA. Association for Computational Linguistics.

Mark Granroth-Wilding and Stephen Clark. 2016. What Happens Next? Event Prediction Using a Compositional Neural Network Model. In *Proceedings of the Thirtieth AAAI Conference on Artificial Intelligence*, AAAI'16, pages 2727–2733. AAAI Press.

Geoffrey Hinton, Nitish Srivastava, and Kevin Swersky. 2012. Overview of mini-batch gradient descent. http://www.cs.toronto.edu/~tijmen/csc321/slides/lecture_slides_lec6.pdf.

Mohit Iyyer, Anupam Guha, Snigdha Chaturvedi, Jordan Boyd-Graber, and Hal Daumé III. 2016. Feuding families and former friends: Unsupervised learning for dynamic fictional relationships. In *Proceedings of the 2016 Conference of the North American Chapter of the Association for Computational Linguistics: Human Language Technologies*, pages 1534–1544, San Diego, California, June. Association for Computational Linguistics.

Diederik Kingma and Jimmy Ba. 2015. Adam: A method for stochastic optimization. In *The International Conference on Learning Representations (ICLR)*, San Diego, May.

Ryan Kiros, Yukun Zhu, Ruslan R Salakhutdinov, Richard Zemel, Raquel Urtasun, Antonio Torralba, and Sanja Fidler. 2015. Skip-thought vectors. In C. Cortes, N. D. Lawrence, D. D. Lee, M. Sugiyama, and R. Garnett, editors, *Advances in Neural Information Processing Systems 28*, pages 3294–3302. Curran Associates, Inc.

Boyang Li, Stephen Lee-Urban, George Johnston, and Mark O. Riedl. 2013. Story generation with crowdsourced plot graphs. In *Proceedings of the Twenty-Seventh AAAI Conference on Artificial Intelligence*, AAAI'13, pages 598–604. AAAI Press.

Zhiyi Luo, Yuchen Sha, Kenny Q. Zhu, Seung-won Hwang, and Zhongyuan Wang. 2016. Commonsense causal reasoning between short texts. In *Proceedings of the Fifteenth International Conference on Principles of Knowledge Representation and Reasoning*, KR'16, pages 421–430. AAAI Press.

Neil McIntyre and Mirella Lapata. 2009. Learning to tell tales: A data-driven approach to story generation. In *Proceedings of the Joint Conference of the 47th Annual Meeting of the ACL and the 4th International Joint Conference on Natural Language Processing of the AFNLP*, pages 217–225, Suntec, Singapore, August. Association for Computational Linguistics.

James R. Meehan. 1977. Tale-spin, an interactive program that writes stories. In *Proceedings of the 5th International Joint Conference on Artificial Intelligence - Volume 1*, IJCAI'77, pages 91–98, San Francisco, CA, USA. Morgan Kaufmann Publishers Inc.

Tomas Mikolov, Martin Karafiat, Lukas Burget, Jan Cernocky, and Sanjeev Khudanpur. 2010. Recurrent Neural Network based language model. In *Proceedings of the 11th Annual Conference of the International Speech Communication Association*, INTERSPEECH 2010, pages 1045–1048.

Tomas Mikolov, Ilya Sutskever, Kai Chen, Greg Corrado, and Jeffrey Dean. 2013. Distributed representations of words and phrases and their compositionality. In *Proceedings of the 26th International Conference on Neural Information Processing Systems*, NIPS'13, pages 3111–3119, USA. Curran Associates Inc.

Nasrin Mostafazadeh, Nathanael Chambers, Xiaodong He, Devi Parikh, Dhruv Batra, Lucy Vanderwende, Pushmeet Kohli, and James Allen. 2016. A corpus and cloze evaluation for deeper understanding of commonsense stories. In *Proceedings of the 2016 Conference of the North American Chapter of the Association for Computational Linguistics: Human Language Technologies*, pages 839–849, San Diego, California, June. Association for Computational Linguistics.

Karl Pichotta and Raymond J. Mooney. 2016. Learning statistical scripts with lstm recurrent neural networks. In *Proceedings of the Thirtieth AAAI Conference on Artificial Intelligence*, AAAI'16, pages 2800–2806. AAAI Press.

Melissa Roemmele, Cosmin Adrian Bejan, and Andrew S. Gordon. 2011. Choice of Plausible Alternatives : An Evaluation of Commonsense Causal Reasoning. *AAAI Spring Symposium: Logical Formalizations of Commonsense Reasoning*, pages 90–95, March.

Ilya Sutskever, James Martens, and Geoffrey Hinton.
2011. Generating text with recurrent neural networks. In Lise Getoor and Tobias Scheffer, editors,
*Proceedings of the 28th International Conference
on Machine Learning (ICML-11)*, ICML '11, pages
1017–1024, New York, NY, USA, June. ACM.

Reid Swanson and Andrew S. Gordon. 2012. Say anything: Using textual case-based reasoning to enable
open-domain interactive storytelling. *ACM Trans.
Interact. Intell. Syst.*, 2(3):16:1–16:35, September.

IIT (BHU): System Description for LSDSem'17 Shared Task

Pranav Goel and **Anil Kumar Singh**
Department of Computer Science and Engineering
Indian Institute of Technology (BHU), Varanasi, India
{pranav.goel.cse14, aksingh.cse}@iitbhu.ac.in

Abstract

This paper describes an ensemble system submitted as part of the LSDSem Shared Task 2017 - the Story Cloze Test. The main conclusion from our results is that an approach based on semantic similarity alone may not be enough for this task. We test various approaches and compare them with two ensemble systems. One is based on voting and the other on logistic regression based classifier. Our final system is able to outperform the previous state of the art for the Story Cloze test. Another very interesting observation is the performance of sentiment based approach which works almost as well on its own as our final ensemble system.

1 Introduction

The Story Cloze Test (Mostafazadeh et al., 2016) is a recently introduced framework to evaluate story understanding and script learning. Representation of commonsense knowledge is major theme in Natural Language Processing and is also important for this task. The organizers provide a training corpus called the ROCStories dataset (we will refer to it as the Story Cloze corpus or dataset). It consists of very simple 98161 everyday life stories (combining the spring and winter training sets). All stories consist of five sentences which capture 'causal and temporal common sense relations between daily events'. The validation and test sets contain 1871 samples each, where each sample contains the first four sentences (the context) of the story, and the system has to complete the story by choosing the fifth sentence (the correct ending) out of the two alternatives provided.

Some of the approaches described in (Mostafazadeh et al., 2016) are used as it

is in our system, while some approaches not tried before in the context of this task (to the best of our knowledge) also form parts of our final ensemble models. Most approaches tried before and also in our experiments rely directly or indirectly on the idea of using semantic similarity of the context and the ending to make the decision. The results point to the conclusion that semantic similarity (at least on its own) may be inadequate as an approach for the Story Cloze test.

Our final system is an ensemble combining the different approaches we tried. It achieves an accuracy of 60.45 on the test set.

The paper is structured as follows. The next section describes various experiments and approaches we tried. Section 3 describes how the different approaches come together to form the system we submitted. Section 4 looks at the various results and draws inferences to make our point. Section 5 presents a small error analysis. Finally, Section 6 presents the conclusions and discusses possible future work.

2 Approaches

We tried five different approaches, out of which four are directly or indirectly utilizing the idea of semantic similarity between the context and the ending. Some past approaches are mentioned here again to enable readers to view them as semantic similarity based approaches, and to use their performance in our observations and conclusion. We give a brief description of our experiments below. The results (performance measured using accuracy which is simply the correct cases divided by the total number of test cases) of all the separate approaches are presented in Table 1.

1. **Gensim (Average Word2Vec):** Chooses the hypothesis with the closest average word2vec (Mikolov et al., 2013) embedding

Proceedings of the 2nd Workshop on Linking Models of Lexical, Sentential and Discourse-level Semantics, pages 81–86,
Valencia, Spain, April 3, 2017. ©2017 Association for Computational Linguistics

to the average word2vec embedding of the context. The concept of semantic similarity is at the very center of this approach. We tried three different variations of this approach:

a) **Training on the Story Cloze training corpus:** This is the same as in (Mostafazadeh et al., 2016) except that we train on the winter training set as well, which makes the corpus size about two times the one used previously. Removing the stop words, keeping a context window of 10 words and vector dimensionality of 300 gave us the results reported in Table 1.

b) **Training on Google news corpus:** Google has released its pre-trained word vectors, trained on a news corpus with a vocabulary of about three million words, which is much larger than the Story Cloze corpus (which contains about 35k unique words). Thus, we decided to explore if the larger set could potentially result in better representation and performance.

c) **Learning the representation of a potential connective word between the context and the ending**: The idea is that a connective with a particular 'sense' (probably temporal or causal in the Story Cloze training set) could perfectly link the context and the ending. We modified all the stories such that a manually introduced symbol (like 'CCC': not in the vocabulary) separates the first four sentences from the fifth sentence, and its representation is learned by training a word2vec model on the data. On the test and validation set, the hypothesis whose representation is the closest to the sum of the vectors of the context and the connective symbol is chosen as the prediction. The intuition comes from the implicit connective sense classification task for the Shallow Discourse Parsing problem (Xue et al., 2015). Context window size 100 and dimensionality 300 were found to be the optimal hyperparameters in our experiments.

Combining the above three – called word2vec (combined) approach – through simple voting produced slightly better results than with any individual variation (as can be seen in Table 1), and thus we used this combined approach in our ensemble model.

2. **Skip-thoughts Model:** The skip-thoughts model's (Kiros et al., 2015) sentence embedding of the context and the alternatives is again compared like the Gensim model, and thus this approach also revolves around semantic similarity.

3. **Gensim Doc2Vec:** Distributed representation of documents and sentences extends the concept of word vectors to larger textual units (Le and Mikolov, 2014). A host of variations were tried (as provided by Python's Gensim functionality (Řehůřek and Sojka, 2010)). The distributed bag of words model (dbow) along with a context window of three words was found to give the best results for this approach (Table 1). This approach is again trying to model semantic similarity via sentence embedding.

4. **Siamese LSTM:** We also implement a deep neural network model for assessing the semantic similarity between a pair of sentences. It uses a Siamese adaptation of the Long Short-Term Memory (LSTM) network (Mueller and Thyagarajan, 2016). The model is implemented as in the paper - using the SICK training set and Google word2vec, with the weights optimized as per the SemEval 2014 task on semantic similarity of sentences (Marelli et al., 2014). This is one of the current state of the art models for capturing semantic similarity.

5. **Sentiment:** In this approach, we choose the hypothesis that matches the average sentiment of the context. We use NLTK VADER Sentiment Analyzer (Hutto and Gilbert, 2014) instead of the Stanford Core NLP tool for sentiment analysis by (Manning et al., 2014) as used in (Mostafazadeh et al., 2016) due to notably better results (Table 1). In our experiments on the validation set, matching sentiment of the full context instead of just the last one/two/three sentence(s) gives the best performance for this approach. This approach does not use semantic similarity.

3 The Ensemble Model

We tried various ways of combining the power of the different approaches, comparing the perfor-

	Story cloze	Google word vectors	Gensim word2vec Using potential connective rep.	Combined	Skip-thoughts	Gensim doc2vec	Siamese LSTM	Sentiment
Validation	0.58	0.577	0.571	0.593	0.536	0.547	0.549	**0.608**
Test	0.571	0.568	0.576	**0.584**	0.552	0.546	0.551	0.582
	0.539	-	-	-	0.552	-	-	0.522

Table 1: Results for individual approaches (last row represents results on the test set for corresponding approach in (Mostafazadeh et al., 2016)

	Approaches involving semantic similarity (logistic regression on validation set)	All approaches (includes sentiment)		Baseline
		Weighted majority voting (Final system submission for validation set spring 2016)	Logistic regression on validation set (Final system submission for test set spring 2016)	
Validation	-	**0.626**	-	0.604
Test	0.587	0.601	**0.605**	0.585

Table 2: Results for the best ensemble models

mances of each on the validation set. This creation of an 'ensemble' model was also tried without using the sentiment approach, so as to observe the best possible performance when only our approaches which involve semantic similarity are combined. We report only the best performing combinations (out of all possible combinations of approaches reported above) here:

a) **Voting based ensemble:** We use weighted majority voting, with prediction from sentiment approach counted twice, and predictions from Siamese LSTM, word2vec (combined) and doc2vec counted once each. The idea is to improve the performance of sentiment approach (the best individual performer) by changing its prediction when all the other three approaches predict a different ending. It may be noted that such voting based methods did not lead to improvement (over combined word2vec) when combinations of only semantic similarity based approaches were used.

b) **Applying a supervised machine learning algorithm:** We used the predictions from sentiment, Siamese LSTM and word2vec (combined) approaches on the validation set as features, with the actual validation set labels as targets and train a machine learning classifier on them. Then this classifier predicts the test set labels (with the same set of features created for test set). Logistic re-

gression (C=0.1) gave the best performance in this method (more than decision tree based methods and naive bayes, and also slightly better than SVM for test as well as validation data). This is the system which formed our final submission. Additionally, combining predictions of doc2vec, word2vec, skip-thoughts, and Siamese LSTM in the exact same way gave us the best performance in the case of using only semantic similarity based approaches (see Table 2).

Baseline: We compare our submitted system with the best performing model on the ROCStories dataset for the Story Cloze task (Mostafazadeh et al., 2016) in Table 2.

4 Results and Discussion

We discuss insights and observations gained from the results of our ensemble system and of the individual approaches obtained on the Story Cloze validation and test sets.

1. **Word vectors:** From Table 1, we can see that word vectors on the Story Cloze corpus perform slightly better than the ones pre-trained on Google news corpus, which has a much larger vocabulary (almost 100 times). This shows that the nature or the domain of the training data really matters for this task. So,

further increase in the Story Cloze training data itself may help by giving us better representations. However, comparing with results in (Mostafazadeh et al., 2016), doubling the size of training set results in about 3-4% increase in performance (Table 1). For further increase, trying different approaches might be better.

2. **Improved performance of the sentiment approach:** For the sentiment approach, using NLTK VADER sentiment analyzer tool for getting polarity scores works notably better by outperforming the Stanford Core NLP (Manning et al., 2014) tool used in (Mostafazadeh et al., 2016) by about 6-7% (the last column of Table 1). As discussed in (Hutto and Gilbert, 2014), the VADER tool is about as accurate in most domains and optimal for the social media domain while being quite simple and more efficient. It happens to work surprisingly well in the context of this task though we do not conclude that it is a better approach as compared to (Socher et al., 2013) approach to sentiment analysis as utilized in Stanford Core NLP tool in general.

3. **General performance:** Our best system (ensemble of sentiment and various semantic similarity based approaches) outperforms the previous best system (using DSSM, as given in (Mostafazadeh et al., 2016)) by about 2% (accuracy on both validation and test sets) (refer to Table 2). Most of the individual approaches (Table 1) show performance that hovers around 60% accuracy (or below). Since they are basically all based on semantic similarity (except the sentiment base approach), the results indicate that we may need to approach the Story Cloze test from a very different direction.

4. **Semantic vs. sentiment similarity:** We can see from Table 1 that the simple sentiment based approach basically outperforms all the semantic similarity based approaches. Even combining those approaches seems barely better than just the sentiment approach (Table 2). This could indicate either the lack of effectiveness of semantic similarity or the fact that sentiment based approach is quite effective. Since our sentiment based approach does not rely on training corpus and

is unlikely to improve with more data (since no learning is involved), we are inclined towards the former inference: Semantic similarity alone may not be enough for the Story Cloze test.

5. **Negative results of the Siamese LSTM:** Siamese LSTM is a deep neural network trained to capture semantic similarity and gave state of the art results on the data for SemEval 2014 shared task on semantic similarity. However, it does not perform well for this task, supporting our conclusion.

6. **Insignificant boost in performance by ensemble system:** Our final ensemble model (Table 2, last column) offers hardly any improvement over the individual sentiment approach (Table 1, last column). This may indicate that the sentiment and semantic similarity based approaches are not complementary.

5 Error Analysis

Table 3 shows examples where our final ensemble system (the one we submitted for test set) and all the individual approaches (as per table 1) simultaneously chose the wrong ending. We believe that a better understanding of commonsense and a good sense of which alternative is the *logical conclusion* based not only on semantic similarity or sentiment, but the temporal aspect of the chain of events as well as plot consistency is missing. In the first example, the model needs to understand that the first three sentences constitute a 'prejudice', and how becoming friends with Sal, who is the target of the prejudice, could lead to the protagonist (Franny) doubting her biased opinion. In the second example, once again, the model would need to understand that the context probably means a nice and happy day for Feliciano, which requires some world knowledge and the sense that spending time like that with a loved one (the grandmother) should lead to happiness. Both the incorrectly chosen endings are inconsistent with the last sentence of the context – Franny being deported – does not make semantic sense when she liked the immigrant, and was not the immigrant herself (we know that the immigrant would get deported and not Franny by our commonsense), while it would not make temporal sense for Feliciano to go picking olives after already collecting them and coming back home to eat with his grandmother.

Context	Incorrect Ending	Correct Ending
Franny did not particularly like all of the immigration happening. She thought immigrants were coming to cause social problems. Franny was upset when an immigrant moved in next door. The immigrant, Sal, was kind and became friends with Franny.	Franny ended up getting deported.	Franny learned to examine her prejudices.
Feliciano went olive picking with his grandmother. While they picked, she told him stories of his ancestors. Before he realized it, the sun was going down. They took the olives home and ate them together.	The pair then went out to pick olives.	Feliciano was happy about his nice day.

Table 3: Examples of stories incorrectly predicted by our model as well as all individual approaches

It is interesting to note how the sentiment approach fails in both the examples. NLTK Vader rates 'getting deported' as neutral while giving a highly negative rating for 'prejudice'. The context is only slightly negative, since the positivity in the last sentence (which talks about Sal being 'nice' and the act of 'becoming friends') offsets the negativity of the previous sentences somewhat. We can see that perhaps the very use of sentiment is not appropriate for example 1. In example 2, the context and the incorrect ending are both neutral, while the correct ending is very positive, hence similarity in sentiment gives an error, but realizing that the context would give rise to a positive ending would have worked.

6   Conclusions and Future Work

We described our submitted system for the Story Cloze test, which combines simple sentiment based approach with a variety of semantic similarity based methods. By highlighting individual and ensemble model results as well as the observations arising from them, we have tried to establish the apparent lack of effectiveness of solely semantic similarity based approaches for this task. This is validated by various experiments and especially the performance of the current state of the art approach for semantic similarity (Siamese LSTM).

Also, an effective future approach should probably be more sophisticated than our sentiment based approach, which does not learn from the training data in any way.

We do not claim that semantic similarity or sentiment based approaches are of no help as they may certainly complement the performances of future approaches. However, they do not seem to be enough on their own, though it is certainly possible that some other semantic similarity based models designed for the Story Cloze training set perform better than our approaches.

While word vectors, sentiment based approach and skip-thoughts sentence embeddings had already been discussed as possible approaches before, we also look at two approaches which have not been tried before for this task, namely Siamese LSTM and Gensim Doc2Vec.

For our future work, we plan to build better ensemble methods. Another idea we are keen to try is logical entailment, since the context entails the ending, and a model which can detect this effectively should be able to predict the right ending (our observations of the validation set make it clear that the context would certainly not be entailing a wrong hypothesis).

References

Clayton J. Hutto and Eric Gilbert. 2014. Vader: A parsimonious rule-based model for sentiment analysis of social media text. In *Proceeding of Eighth International AAAI Conference on Weblogs and Social Media*.

Ryan Kiros, Yukun Zhu, Ruslan R. Salakhutdinov, Richard Zemel, Raquel Urtasun, Antonio Torralba, and Sanja Fidler. 2015. Skip-thought vectors. In *Proceedings of Advances in neural information processing systems*, pages 3294–3302.

Quoc V. Le and Tomas Mikolov. 2014. Distributed representations of sentences and documents. In *Proceeding of ICML*, volume 14, pages 1188–1196.

Christopher D. Manning, Mihai Surdeanu, John Bauer, Jenny Rose Finkel, Steven Bethard, and David McClosky. 2014. The stanford corenlp natural language processing toolkit. In *Proceedings of the ACL (System Demonstrations)*, pages 55–60.

Marco Marelli, Luisa Bentivogli, Marco Baroni, Raffaella Bernardi, Stefano Menini, and Roberto Zamparelli. 2014. Semeval-2014 task 1: Evaluation of compositional distributional semantic models on full sentences through semantic relatedness and textual entailment. In *Proceedings of the 8th International Workshop on Semantic Evaluation (SemEval)*.

Tomas Mikolov, Ilya Sutskever, Kai Chen, Greg S. Corrado, and Jeff Dean. 2013. Distributed representations of words and phrases and their compositionality. In *Proceeding of Advances in neural information processing systems*, pages 3111–3119.

Nasrin Mostafazadeh, Nathanael Chambers, Xiaodong He, Devi Parikh, Dhruv Batra, Lucy Vanderwende, Pushmeet Kohli, and James Allen. 2016. A corpus and cloze evaluation for deeper understanding of commonsense stories. In *Proceedings of NAACL-HLT*, pages 839–849.

Jonas Mueller and Aditya Thyagarajan. 2016. Siamese recurrent architectures for learning sentence similarity. In *Proceeding of AAAI*, pages 2786–2792.

Radim Řehůřek and Petr Sojka. 2010. Software Framework for Topic Modelling with Large Corpora. In *Proceedings of the LREC 2010 Workshop on New Challenges for NLP Frameworks*, pages 45–50, Valletta, Malta, May. ELRA. `http://is.muni.cz/publication/884893/en`.

Richard Socher, Alex Perelygin, Jean Y. Wu, Jason Chuang, Christopher D. Manning, Andrew Y. Ng, Christopher Potts, et al. 2013. Recursive deep models for semantic compositionality over a sentiment treebank. In *Proceedings of the conference on empirical methods in natural language processing (EMNLP)*, volume 1631, page 1642. Citeseer.

Nianwen Xue, Hwee Tou Ng, Sameer Pradhan, Rashmi Prasad, Christopher Bryant, and Attapol Rutherford. 2015. The conll-2015 shared task on shallow discourse parsing. In *Proceedings of the CoNLL Shared Task*, pages 1–16.

Story Cloze Ending Selection Baselines and Data Examination

Todor Mihaylov
Research Training Group AIPHES
Institute for Computational Linguistics
Heidelberg University
mihaylov@cl.uni-heidelberg.de

Anette Frank
Research Training Group AIPHES
Institute for Computational Linguistics
Heidelberg University
frank@cl.uni-heidelberg.de

Abstract

This paper describes two supervised baseline systems for the Story Cloze Test Shared Task (Mostafazadeh et al., 2016a). We first build a classifier using features based on word embeddings and semantic similarity computation. We further implement a neural LSTM system with different encoding strategies that try to model the relation between the story and the provided endings. Our experiments show that a model using representation features based on average word embedding vectors over the given story words and the candidate ending sentences words, joint with similarity features between the story and candidate ending representations performed better than the neural models. Our best model achieves an accuracy of 72.42, ranking 3rd in the official evaluation.

1 Introduction

Understanding common sense stories is an easy task for humans but represents a challenge for machines. A recent common sense story understanding task is the 'Story Cloze Test' (Mostafazadeh et al., 2016a), where a human or an AI system has to read a given four-sentence story and select the proper ending out of two proposed endings. While the majority class baseline performance on the given test set yields an accuracy of 51.3%, human performance achieves 100%. This makes the task a good challenge for an AI system. The Story Cloze Test task is proposed as a Shared Task for LSDSem 2017[1]. 17 teams registered for the Shared Task and 10 teams submitted their results[2].

Our contribution is that we set a new baseline for the task, showing that a simple linear model based on distributed representations and semantic similarity features achieves state-of-the-art results. We also evaluate the ability of different embedding models to represent common knowledge required for this task. We present an LSTM-based classifier with different representation encodings that tries to model the relation between the story and alternative endings and argue about its inability to do so.

2 Task description and data construction

The Story Cloze Test is a natural language understanding task that consists in selecting the right ending for a given short story. The evaluation data consists of a *Dev set* and a *Test set*, each containing samples of four sentences of a story, followed by two alternative sentences, from which the system has to select the proper story ending. An example of such a story is presented in Table 1.

The instances in the *Dev* and *Test* gold data sets (1871 instances each) were crowd-sourced together with the related ROC Stories corpus (Mostafazadeh et al., 2016a). The ROC stories consists of around 100,000 crowd-sourced short five sentence stories ranging over various topics. These stories do not feature a wrong ending, but with appropriate extensions they can be deployed as training data for the Story Cloze task.

Task modeling. We approach the task as a supervised classification problem. For every classification instance *(Story, Ending1, Ending2)* we predict one of the labels in Label=\{*Good,Bad*\}.

Obtaining a small training set from *Dev* set. We construct a (small) training data set from the *Dev* set by splitting it randomly into a *Dev-Train* and a *Dev-Dev* set containing 90% and 10% of the

---

[1] Workshop on Linking Models of Lexical, Sentential and Discourse-level Semantics 2017

[2] https://competitions.codalab.org/competitions/15333 - Story Cloze Test at CodaLab

Proceedings of the 2nd Workshop on Linking Models of Lexical, Sentential and Discourse-level Semantics, pages 87–92,
Valencia, Spain, April 3, 2017. ©2017 Association for Computational Linguistics

Story context	Good Ending	Bad ending
Mary and Emma drove to the beach. They decided to swim in the ocean. Mary turned to talk to Emma. Emma said to watch out for the waves.	A big wave knocked Mary down.	The ocean was a calm as a bathtub.

Table 1: Example of a given story with a bad and a good ending.

original *Dev* set. From each instance in *Dev-Train* we generate 2 instances by swapping *Ending1* and *Ending2* and inversing the class label.

Generating training data from ROC stories. We also make use of the ROC Stories corpus in order to generate a large training data set. We experiment with three methods:

(i.) Random endings. For each story we employ the first 4 sentences as the story context. We use the original ending as *Good* ending and define a *Bad* ending by randomly choosing some ending from an alternative story in the corpus. From each story with one *Good* ending we generate 10 *Bad* examples by selecting 10 random endings.

(ii.) Coherent stories and endings with common participants and noun arguments. Given that some random story endings are too clearly unconnected to the story, here we aim to select *Bad* candidate endings that are coherent with the story, yet still distinct from a *Good* ending. To this end, for each story in the ROC Stories corpus, we obtain the lemmas of all pronouns (tokens with part of speech tag starting with 'PR') and lemmas of all nouns (tokens with part of speech tag starting with 'NN') and select the top 10 endings from other stories that share most of these features as *Bad* endings.

(iii.) Random coherent stories and endings. We also modify (ii.) so that we select the nearest 500 endings to the story context and select 10 randomly.

3 A Baseline Method

For tackling the problem of right story ending selection we follow a feature-based classification approach that was previously applied to bi-clausal classification tasks in (Mihaylov and Frank, 2016; Mihaylov and Nakov, 2016). It uses features based on word embeddings to represent the clauses and semantic similarity measured between these representations for the clauses. Here, we adopt this approach to model parts of the story and the candidate endings. For the given *Story* and the given

candidate *Endings* we extract features based on word embeddings. An advantage of this approach is that it is fast for training and that it only requires pre-trained word embeddings as an input.

3.1 Features

In our models we only deploy features based on word embedding vectors. We are using two types of features: (i) **representation features** that model the semantics of parts of the story using word embedding vectors, and (ii) **similarity scores** that capture specific properties of the relation holding between the story and its candidate endings. For computing similarity between the embedding representations of the story components, we employ cosine similarity.

The different feature types are described below.

(i) Embedding representations for *Story* and *Ending*. For each *Story* (sentences 1 to 4) and story endings *Ending1* and *Ending2* we construct a centroid vector from the embedding vectors $\vec{w_i}$ of all words w_i in their respective surface yield.

(ii.) Story to Ending Semantic Vector Similarities. We calculate various similarity features on the basis of the centroid word vectors for all or selected sentences in the given *Story* and the *Ending1* and *Ending2* sentences, as well as on parts of the these sentences:

Story to Ending similarity. We assume that a given *Story* and its *Good Ending* are connected by a specific semantic relation or some piece of common sense knowledge. Their representation vectors should thus stand in a specific similarity relation to each other. We use their cosine similarity as a feature. Similarity between the story sentences and a candidate ending has already been proposed as a baseline by Mostafazadeh et al. (2016b) but it does not perform well as a single feature.

Maximized similarity. This measure ranks each word in the *Story* according to its similarity with the centroid vector of *Ending*, and we compute the average similarity for the top-ranked N

words. We chose the similarity scores of the top 1,2,3 and 5 words as features. Our assumption is that the average similarity between the *Story* representation and the top N most similar words in the *Ending* might characterize the proper ending as the *Good* ending. We also extract **maximized aligned similarity**. For each word in *Story*, we choose the most similar word from the yield of *Ending* and take the average of all best word pair similarities, as suggested in Tran et al. (2015).

Part of speech (POS) based word vector similarities. For each sentence in the given four sentence story and the candidate endings we performed part of speech tagging using the Stanford CoreNLP (Manning et al., 2014) parser, and computed similarities between centroid vectors of words with a specific tag from *Story* and the centroid vector of *Ending*. Extracted features for POS similarities include symmetric and asymmetric combinations: for example we calculate the similarity between *Nouns* from *Story* with *Nouns* from *Ending* and similarity between *Nouns* from *Story* with *Verbs* from *Ending* and vice versa.

The assumption is that embeddings for some parts of speech between *Story* and *Ending* might be closer to those of other parts of speech for the *Good* ending of a given story.

3.2 Classifier settings

For our feature-based approach we concatenate the extracted representation and similarity features in a feature vector, scale their values to the 0 to 1 range, and feed the vectors to a classifier. We train and evaluate a L2-regularized Logistic Regression classifier with the LIBLINEAR (Fan et al., 2008) solver as implemented in *scikit-learn* (Pedregosa et al., 2011).

For each separate experiment we tune the regularization parameter C with 5 fold cross-validation on the *Dev* set and then train a new model on the entire *Dev* set in order to evaluate on the *Test* set.

4   Neural LSTM Baseline Method

We compare our feature-based linear classifier baseline to a neural approach. Our goal is to explore a simple neural method and to investigate how well it performs with the given small dataset. We implement a Long Short-Term Memory (LSTM) (Hochreiter and Schmidhuber, 1997) recurrent neural network model.

4.1   Representations

We are using the raw LSTM output of the encoder. We also experiment with an encoder with attention to model the relation between a story and a candidate ending, following (Rocktäschel et al., 2015).

(i) Raw LSTM representations.   For each given instance *(Story, Ending1, Ending2)* we first encode the *Story* token word vector representations using a recurrent neural network (RNN) with long short-term memory (LSTM) units. We use the last output $\mathbf{h}_L^s$ and $\mathbf{c}_L^s$ states of the *Story* to initialize the first LSTM cells for the respective encodings $\mathbf{e}_1$ and $\mathbf{e}_2$ of *Ending1* and *Ending2*, where $\mathbf{L}$ is the token length of the *Story* sequence.

We build the final representation $\mathbf{o}_{se1e2}$ by concatenating the $\mathbf{e}_1$ and $\mathbf{e}_2$ representations. Finally, for classification we use a softmax layer over the output $\mathbf{o}_{se1e2}$ by mapping it into the target space of the two classes (Good, Bad) using a parameter matrix $\mathbf{M}_o$ and bias $\mathbf{b}_o$ as given in (Eq.1). We train using the cross-entropy loss.

$$label_{prob} = softmax(W^o o_{se1e2} + b_o) \quad (1)$$

(ii) Attention-based representations   We also model the relation h^* between the *Story* and each of the *Endings* using the attention-weighted representation $\mathbf{r}$ between the last token output $\mathbf{h}_N^e$ of the *Ending* representation and each of the token representations $[\mathbf{h}_1^s..\mathbf{h}_L^s]$ of the *Story*, strictly following the attention definition by Rocktäschel et al. (2015). The final representation for each ending is presented by Eq.2, where $\mathbf{W}^p$ and $\mathbf{W}^x$ are trained projection matrices.

$$h^* = tanh(W^p r + W^x h_N^e) \quad (2)$$

We then present the output representation $\mathbf{o}_{se1e2}$ as a concatenation of the encoded *Ending1* and *Ending2* representations h_{e1}^* and h_{e2}^* and use Eq.1 to obtain the output label likelihood.

(iii) Combined raw LSTM output and attention representation   We also perform experiments with combined LSTM outputs and representations. In this setting we present the output $\mathbf{o}_{se1e2}$ as presented in Eq.3:

$$o_{se1e2} = concat(e_1, h_{e1}^*, e_2, h_{e2}^*) \quad (3)$$

4.2   Model Parameters and Tuning

We perform experiments with configurations of the model using grid search on the batch size (50,

System	Accuracy
Human	100.00
msap	75.20
cogcomp	74.39
Our features baseline	**72.42**
Our neural system	**72.10**
ukp	71.67
DSSM	58.50
Skip-thoughts sim	55.20
Word2Vec sim	53.90
Majority baseline	51.30

Table 2: Comparison of our models to shared task participants' results and other baselines. *Word2Vec sim*, *Skip-thoughts sim* and *DSSM* are described in (Mostafazadeh et al., 2016b).

100, 200, 300, 400, 500) and LSTM output size (128, 256, 384, 512), by training a simple model with raw LSTM encoding on *Dev-Train* and evaluating on the *Dev-Dev*. For each configuration we train 5 models and take the parameters of the best. The best result on the *Dev-Dev* set is achieved for LSTM with output size 384 and batch Size 500 after 7 epochs and achieves accuracy of 72.10 on the official *Test*. For learning rate optimization we use Adam optimizer (Kingma and Ba, 2015) with initial learning rate 0.001.

Parameter initialization. We initialize the LSTM weights with Xavier initialization (Glo, 2010) and bias with a constant zero vector.

5   Experiments and Results

Overall results. In Table 2 we compare our best systems to existing baselines, Shared Task participant systems[3] and human performance. *Our features baseline* system is our best feature-based system using embeddings and *word2vec* trained on *Dev* and tuned with cross-validation. *Our neural system* employs raw LSTM encodings as described in Section 4.1(i) and it is trained on the *Dev-Dev* dataset which consists of 90% of the *Dev* dataset selected randomly and tuned on the rest of *Dev*. The best result in the task is achieved by Schwartz et al. (2017) *(msap)* who employ stylistic features combined with RNN representations. We have no information about *cogcomp* and *ukp*.

Model variations and experiments. The Story Cloze Test is a story understanding problem. However, the given stories are very short and they require background knowledge about relations between the given entities, entity types and events defining the story and their endings, as well as relations between these events. We first train our feature-based model with alternative embedding representations in order to select the best source of knowledge for further experiments.

We experiment with different word embedding models pre-trained on a large number of tokens including *word2vec*[4] (Mikolov et al., 2013), *GloVe* (Pennington et al., 2014) and *ConceptNet Numberbatch* (Speer and Chin, 2016). Results on training the feature-based model with different word embeddings are shown in Table 3. The results indicate how well the vector representation models perform in terms of encoding common sense stories. We present the performance of the embedding models depending on the defined features. We perform feature ablation experiments to determine the features which contribute most to the overall score for the different models. Using *All* features defined in Section 3.1, the word2vec vectors, trained on Google News 100B corpus perform best followed by ConcepNet enriched embeddings and Glove trained on Common Crawl 840B. The word2vec model suffers most when similarity features are excluded. We note that the ConceptNet embeddings do not decrease performance when similarity features are excluded, unlike all other models. We also see that the *POS similarities* are more important than the *MaxSim* and the *Sim (cosine betwen all words in Story and Ending)* as they yield worse results, for almost all models, when excluded from *All* features.

In column *WE E1, E2* we report results on features based only on *Ending1* and *Ending 2*. We note that the overall results are still very good. From this we can derive that the difference of *Good vs. Bad* endings is not only defined in the story context but it is also characterized by the information present in these sentences in isolation. This could be due to a reporting bias (Gordon and Van Durme, 2013) employed by the crowdworkers in the corpus construction process.

The last column *Sims only* shows results with features based only on similarity features. It in-

---

[3]https://competitions.codalab.org/competitions/15333 - The Story Cloze Test Shared Task home page

[4]https://code.google.com/archive/p/word2vec/ - Pre-trained embeddings on Google News dataset (100B words).

Model	All	All wo POS sim	All wo MaxSim	All wo Sim	WE S, E1, E2+Sim	WE E1, E2	Sims only
Word2Vec GN 100B 300d	**72.42**	71.41	71.94	72.10	71.51	70.71	58.15
Concepnet 300d	72.05	**72.05**	**72.05**	72.05	**71.83**	**71.67**	61.67
Glove 840B 300d	71.41	71.09	71.89	**72.26**	70.82	70.71	60.28
Glove 6B 200d	69.43	69.75	68.31	69.64	68.04	68.68	**62.37**
Glove 6B 300d	68.84	69.32	69.21	69.05	68.79	68.89	61.19
Glove 6B 100d	68.84	68.09	67.93	68.41	67.66	67.56	60.82
Glove 6B 50d	64.89	66.01	64.19	64.67	64.78	64.83	58.57

Table 3: Experiments using linear classifier with features based on word embeddings. Trained on *Dev* (tuned with cross-validation) and evaluated on *Test*.

Model	Epoch	Dev-Dev	Test
LSTM Raw	7	77.12	72.10
LSTM Raw + Att	2	79.25	68.30
Attention	9	72.79	63.22

Table 4: Comparison between LSTM representation strategies.

cludes all story-to-ending semantic vector similarities described in Section 3.1.

We also perform experiments with the neural LSTM model. In Table 4 we compare results of the LSTM representation models that we examined for the task. We trained the models on the *Dev-Train* for 10 epochs and take the best performing model on the *Dev-Dev* dataset.

Our best LSTM model uses only raw LSTM encodings of the *Story* and the candidate *Endings*, without using attention. Here the *Attention* representation is intended to capture semantic relations between the *Story* context and the candidate *Endings*, similar to the *Similarities only* setup examined with the feature-based approach. Considering the low performance of *Attention*, the poor results of the *semantic similarity features* and the high performance of the feature-based model with *Ending only* features we hypothesize that the reason for this unexpected result is that the background knowledge presented in the training data is not enough to learn strong relations between the story context and the endings.

Experiments with generated data. We also try to employ the data from the ROC Stories corpus by generating labeled datasets following all approaches described in Section 2. Training our best neural model using all of the generated datasets separately without any further data selection yields results close to the random baseline of the ending selection task. We also try to filter the generated data by training several feature-based and neural models with our best configurations and evaluating the generated data. We take only instances that have been classified correctly by all models. The idea here was to generate much more data (with richer vocabulary) that performs at least as good as the *Dev* data as training. However the results of the models trained on these datasets were not better than the one trained on *Dev* and *Dev-Dev (for the neural models)*.

6 Conclusion and Future work

In this work we built two strong supervised baseline systems for the Story Cloze task: one based on semantic features based on word embedding representations and bi-clausal similarity features obtained from them, and one on based on a neural network LSTM-based encoder model. The neural network approach trained on a small dataset performs worse than the feature-based classifier by a small margin only, and our best model ranks 3rd according to the shared task web page.

In terms of data, it seems that the most important features are coming from word representations trained on large text corpora rather than relations between the data. Also we can train a model that performs well only on the given endings, without a given context which could mean that there is a bias in the annotation process. However, this requires more insights and analysis.

In future work we plan improve the current results on this (or a revised) dataset by collecting more external knowledge and obtaining more or different training data from the original ROC Stories corpus.

Acknowledgments. This work is supported by the German Research Foundation as part of the Research Training Group "Adaptive Preparation of Information from Heterogeneous Sources" (AIPHES) under grant No. GRK 1994/1.

We would like to thank the reviewers for their valuable and constructive comments.

References

Rong-En Fan, Kai-Wei Chang, Cho-Jui Hsieh, Xiang-Rui Wang, and Chih-Jen Lin. 2008. Liblinear: A library for large linear classification. *J. Mach. Learn. Res.*, 9:1871–1874, June.

2010. Understanding the difficulty of training deep feedforward neural networks. *Proceedings of the 13th International Conference on Artificial Intelligence and Statistics (AISTATS)*, 9:249–256.

Jonathan Gordon and Benjamin Van Durme. 2013. Reporting bias and knowledge acquisition. *Proc. 2013 Work. Autom. Knowl. base Constr. - AKBC '13*, (circa):25–30.

Sepp Hochreiter and Jürgen Schmidhuber. 1997. Long short-term memory. *Neural Comput.*, 9(8):1735–1780, November.

Diederik P. Kingma and Jimmy Lei Ba. 2015. Adam: a Method for Stochastic Optimization. *Int. Conf. Learn. Represent. 2015*, pages 1–15.

Christopher D Manning, John Bauer, Jenny Finkel, Steven J Bethard, Mihai Surdeanu, and David Mc-Closky. 2014. The Stanford CoreNLP Natural Language Processing Toolkit. *Proceedings of 52nd Annual Meeting of the Association for Computational Linguistics: System Demonstrations*, pages 55–60.

Todor Mihaylov and Anette Frank. 2016. Discourse Relation Sense Classification Using Cross-argument Semantic Similarity Based on Word Embeddings. In *Proceedings of the Twentieth Conference on Computational Natural Language Learning - Shared Task*, pages 100–107, Berlin, Germany. Association for Computational Linguistics.

Todor Mihaylov and Preslav Nakov. 2016. SemanticZ at SemEval-2016 Task 3: Ranking relevant answers in community question answering using semantic similarity based on fine-tuned word embeddings. In *Proceedings of the 10th International Workshop on Semantic Evaluation*, SemEval '16, San Diego, California, USA.

Tomas Mikolov, Wen-tau Yih, and Geoffrey Zweig. 2013. Linguistic regularities in continuous space word representations. In *Proceedings of the 2013 Conference of the North American Chapter of the Association for Computational Linguistics: Human Language Technologies*, NAACL-HLT '13, pages 746–751, Atlanta, Georgia, USA.

Nasrin Mostafazadeh, Nathanael Chambers, Xiaodong He, Devi Parikh, Dhruv Batra, Lucy Vanderwende, Pushmeet Kohli, and James Allen. 2016a. A Corpus and Evaluation Framework for Deeper Understanding of Commonsense Stories. *Naacl*.

Nasrin Mostafazadeh, Lucy Vanderwende, Wen-tau Yih, Pushmeet Kohli, and James Allen. 2016b. Story cloze evaluator: Vector space representation evaluation by predicting what happens next. In *Proceedings of the 1st Workshop on Evaluating Vector-Space Representations for NLP*, pages 24–29, Berlin, Germany, August. Association for Computational Linguistics.

F. Pedregosa, G. Varoquaux, A. Gramfort, V. Michel, B. Thirion, O. Grisel, M. Blondel, P. Prettenhofer, R. Weiss, V. Dubourg, J. Vanderplas, A. Passos, D. Cournapeau, M. Brucher, M. Perrot, and E. Duchesnay. 2011. Scikit-learn: Machine learning in Python. *Journal of Machine Learning Research*, 12:2825–2830.

Jeffrey Pennington, Richard Socher, and Christopher D Manning. 2014. GloVe: Global Vectors for Word Representation. *Proceedings of the 2014 Conference on Empirical Methods in Natural Language Processing*, pages 1532–1543.

Tim Rocktäschel, Edward Grefenstette, Karl Moritz Hermann, Tomáš Kočiský, and Phil Blunsom. 2015. Reasoning about Entailment with Neural Attention. *Unpublished*, (2015):1–9, sep.

Roy Schwartz, Maarten Sap, Ioannis Konstas, Leila Zilles, Yejin Choi, and Noah A Smith. 2017. The Effect of Different Writing Tasks on Linguistic Style: A Case Study of the ROC Story Cloze Task. *Proc. Link. Model. Lexical, Sentential Discourse-level Semant. Shar. Task*, feb.

Robert Speer and Joshua Chin. 2016. An ensemble method to produce high-quality word embeddings. *arXiv preprint arXiv:1604.01692*.

Quan Hung Tran, Vu Tran, Tu Vu, Minh Nguyen, and Son Bao Pham. 2015. JAIST: Combining multiple features for answer selection in community question answering. In *Proceedings of the 9th International Workshop on Semantic Evaluation*, SemEval '15, pages 215–219, Denver, Colorado, USA.

Author Index

Association for Computational Linguistics
209 N. Eighth Street
Stroudsburg, Pennsylvania 18360

ISBN 978-1-5108-3866-6